The Way of Story

THE CRAFT & SOUL
OF WRITING

CATHERINE ANN JONES

MICHAEL WIESE PRODUCTIONS

Published by Michael Wiese Productions
3940 Laurel Canyon Blvd. – Suite 1111
Studio City, CA 91604
(818) 379-8799, (818) 986-3408 (FAX).
mw@mwp.com
www.mwp.com

Cover design by Barry Grimes, agdesign
Cover photo by Steve McCurry, Magnum Photos
Interior design by William Morosi
Printed by McNaughton & Gunn

Manufactured in the United States of America
Copyright 2007 Catherine Ann Jones

Library of Congress Cataloging-in-Publication Data
Jones, Catherine Ann, 1944-
   The way of story : the craft & soul of writing / Catherine Ann Jones.
      p. cm.
   ISBN 978-1-932907-32-2
   1. Motion picture authorship. 2. Playwriting. 3. Creative writing. I. Title.
   PN1996.J65 2007
   808.3'93--dc22
                                        2007019803

Printed on Recycled stock

The whole of life can be a meditation ... even writing.

— Sri Adwayananda

Contents

Prologue

*I*N THE BEGINNING was story. The cave-
man rushed back to his tribe and
excitedly acted out his encounter with
some Paleolithic beast. This was his story
and forever after he would be remembered
by this story. Stories have a sacred dimension, not because of gods but because a man
or woman's sense of self and her world is
created through them. These stories orient
the life of a people through time, establishing the reality of their world. Thus
meaning and purpose are given to people's
lives. Without story, we do not exist. *The
Way of Story* is how we discover who we are.

Chapter 1

In the Beginning Was Story...

*E*INSTEIN WAS WRONG. "The world is made up of stories, not atoms," as poet Muriel Rukeyser once said. Novelist John Steinbeck in his Nobel Prize acceptance speech remarked that "literature is as old as speech. It grew out of human need for it, and it has not changed except to become more needed." This is no less true today. From Shakespeare to *Star Wars*, from Dante to le Carre, the *way of story* is a journey of discovery forged by discipline and craft. Though it is craft that transforms the initial raw inspiration into form, storytelling begins within, and is as much as part of our past as our genetic structure.

Storytelling is not only the root of film, theatre, literature, and culture, but of the life experience itself. The listener maintains touch with his mythic self and the truths there represented. In losing touch with our myths, there may be a danger of losing touch with ourselves. Today, in modern society, there is a fragmentation which separates most of us from our central core or soul. With all our progress, perhaps something has been lost which earlier cultures knew to value: the soul connection.

Story has been the foundation of rituals that empower both individual and collective values since society began. Story provides both identity and standards to live by and is thus essential for our well-being. It serves as a mirror to reflect who we are and what we believe in. What story would you choose to live by? The answer offers a clue to your soul, your deepest self.

For thirty thousand years and in the earliest forms of oral tradition, shamans have tended the soul. The very word, *shaman*, coming from the Tungus people of Siberia, means excited, moved, raised. He journeys out of body to a realm beyond time and space. The shaman's soul leaves his body in trance state and travels to the underworld or skyward, returning with a message for the community. In this way, the shaman becomes a bridge between the two worlds of earth and spirit. The shaman is an ear for his community. He discovers where their suffering lies, and speaks to that.

What has this to do with us today? We have been split off from spirit since the Industrial Revolution, and today's Age of Information is a poor substitute for the callings of spirit. Information is not — nor was it ever— wisdom. Knowledge is more than the mere naming of names, survival more than material sustenance. Man needs connection with the worlds of both matter and spirit in order to find meaning and balance in life. The integration of matter and spirit is the making of soul or wholeness, which gives meaning to life. Soul combines body, spirit, and mind. In olden times, shamans interpreted psychological illness as separation from soul. The shaman's job then was to retrieve the severed soul and unite it — or return it — to the one possessed or ill.

Is this not what the artist does? Is it possible that today's artist or writer might fill the gap of the missing shaman? As an actress-playwright in New York and later as a screenwriter in Hollywood, I have often wondered if today's dramatist is not carrying the forgotten role of shaman.

As the ancient shaman, so often will the writer descend into the depths of himself in order to return with a message. Though he serves the community, he is more often than not marginal — separate from society. Perhaps this marginality may be necessary in order to move freely between the opposite worlds, unrestrained by society. The artist often suffers from this separateness. Consider Virginia Woolf, Sylvia Plath, Vincent van Gogh, and Jackson Pollack who all opted for suicide in the end — even though the gifts such artists bring will enrich society long after they are gone.

Surely, the dramatist also provides a bridge between the split worlds of matter and spirit. In my play, *On the Edge*, when Vita Sackville-West asks Virginia Woolf how she is, this is her reply:

> On the edge, I'm afraid. The strain, I think of inhabiting two very different worlds. This afternoon, for instance, when I was on my walk. At first, I felt the wet grass on my feet. . . and perhaps a robin sang. But then, I began to be drawn in. The more it drew me, the less touch I had with the concrete world. I was in another universe entirely. I was in myself. And this world seemed far, far more real than the one I had left.

From the early beginnings of Hollywood a century ago, the movie moguls were interested in one thing: the story. "What's the story?" Louis B. Mayer of Metro-Goldwyn-Mayer would ask, "Just tell me the story." Even today, Hollywood executives decide which story will make it to the screen by hearing the story pitched or told to them, rather than having to read it. Also, for better or worse, Hollywood and television have influenced how plays and novels are written. No longer will the reader patiently read fifty pages while waiting for something to happen. Books are chosen by publishers today with an eye to a possible movie sale. This is one of the reasons why today the principles of screenwriting apply to all forms of narrative writing. So, regardless of whether you're writing a memoir, mystery, or novel, in the beginning is the Story...

Award-winning actor and writer William H. Macy (*Fargo*, *Seabiscuit*) commented in the *Los Angeles Times*:

> They can pretty much do anything they want technically now, but they're forgetting to write a story. You've got to keep in mind that audiences universally want one thing: a good story. And special effects make it better, but they can't replace story.

So, what makes a good story? The answer covers all genres (types of story such as drama, comedy, mystery, etc.) and can be revealed in one word: character. It is no accident that the best films or novels are character-driven stories.

For instance, *Gone with the Wind* is not about the Civil War, but about Scarlett O'Hara. The Civil War is merely the venue or backdrop to this great love story. An important point to remember in writing period pieces is that the theme should be universal, that is, as relevant today as when your story takes place. If you wish to write a story about the Civil War, you must write a specific story about specific people. Remember, too, that it is important not to confuse venue with what a story is really about. Your job as author then is to find the story within the story.

It is no accident that many hit films carry the main character in the title. Examples are *Harry Potter and the Goblet of Fire, Forrest Gump, Driving Miss Daisy, Braveheart, Lawrence of Arabia, Dr. Zhivago, The English Patient, and Erin Brockovich.* Character-driven stories allow the readers or audience to identify with one major character who in turn navigates them through the story. So character is vital as the way into the story or plot. (In chapter five, creating character-driven stories will be explored more fully.)

How to choose a story? You've probably been told to write what you know about, right? Wrong! George Lucas never traveled to outer space, yet his original story, *Star Wars*, did rather well. I am often asked by clients and the Way of Story workshop participants, how to choose which story to write. The important guiding line is to choose a story you have a strong emotional connection with. Generally speaking, people go to movies or read in order to feel.

We have today become conditioned, even educated, to think and not to feel. This creates an imbalance both personally and collectively. Consequently, appropriate and inappropriate venues are sought to allow feeling. Reading a book or seeing a movie is an appropriate outlet for this. There is a varied smorgasbord as one can choose a story to feel anger, terror, a sense of power, sexual titillation, romantic love, and so on. Anthony Minghella, director of Oscar winner *The English Patient*, says, "I want to feel in film." So know thyself and you will know what to write about. By this, I simply mean, know what moves you. Child abuse? Political or corporate corruption? The triumph of the human spirit in a hopeless situation? Two unlikely lovers? A search for God?

If the writer chooses a story he feels strongly about, that will be felt, in turn, by the reader or audience. Laura Hillenbrand, the author of the book *Seabiscuit*, suffered several years from chronic fatigue syndrome. She kept on writing and instilled all her feelings of being held down by outer circumstances into the completion of the book. Hence, her own state paralleled the theme of her best-selling book. She had to overcome this condition to complete a book she was struggling to write. She infused the story with her own struggle. The book was called *Seabiscuit*, a true story of three men living during the Depression in America, and their triumph against great odds. Audiences relate to such a life struggle as much now as then. It is contagious. The book became a best seller and was adapted into a major film that received seven Oscar nominations.

Stories written by formulas rarely move us, and consequently fail. They are too generic, not about specific people. This is why true stories are so popular. Knowing the story is true, that it really happened to someone, means it could happen to you. Also, choosing a story that moves you will provide your point of view (POV), so important in a great story. Your perspective becomes a unique voice, mirroring your personal relationship to the material — in other words, how you feel about your characters, story, and theme. In this way, the philosophy and values of the author are revealed through his or her story — regardless of the subject matter. Though the story need not be the details of the writer's own life, the emotional investment in the subject or character will be felt to be real. Emotions derived from all we have lived and felt passionate about become a rich well which every good writer will draw from.

For now, just remember that it is the emotional power of your story that will ultimately determine its success. As a story and script consultant, and judge for the Emmys, Oscars, and various film festivals, I have remained unmoved by convoluted plots depicting car crashes, hospitals, and murders, while being deeply moved by Oscar winner *Brokeback Mountain*, a simple story about two cowboys who form an unusual bond. Why is this? Outer action is not necessarily dramatic action. Dramatic action is what takes place emotionally between people.

It is not what happens in a great story that matters. Rather it is how what happens to your main character affects him and his relationships, and ultimately changes him in some vital way.

Where to find a story? There are as many answers to where to find your story as there are stories. Novelist Truman Capote had a spinster aunt who became immortalized in *A Christmas Memory*, later made into a television movie starring the amazing Geraldine Page. My Southern mother has found her way into at least four of my plays or films, not literally, but as a prototype for various characters. All fiction is autobiography in disguise.

I grew up in New Orleans listening to women's stories. My grandmother would have her friends over for a quilting bee. They would sit in a circle and work on the same quilt, sewing bits and pieces of material into one enduring whole. At the same time, the women would share bits and pieces of their lives with one another which made of their friendships another kind of quilt. I can remember even now myself at the age of five or six sitting on the staircase just around the corner, unseen, mesmerized by these vibrant Southern voices. Eventually, this led to a family play, *The Women of Cedar Creek*. Writing an all-female cast depicting three generations of Southern women was my reply to all the plays — usually written by men — with more male roles than female. Though the starting point of the play was the actual feminine members of my own family, I pushed both character and story to extremes, leaving far behind the bare facts of my own family's history. It is well to remember that good writing is more an impressionist painting than a literal photograph.

One idea for a play came from a secondhand bookstore, the Strand, located on the corner of Twelfth and Broadway in New York City. I was teaching playwriting at The New School University, a few blocks away from the Strand, and would habitually drop by, before or after my class, and browse. One afternoon, I found a slightly tattered copy of a small book, *The Letters of Calamity Jane*. Soon afterwards, I was invited to Ossabaw Island off the coast of Savannah, Georgia to write. The island was like stepping back into the early nineteenth century. No cars, only fifteen people living on an island the size of Manhattan, wild horses roamed freely, and one lone sheriff was the law on the privately owned island. There I wrote *Calamity Jane*, set in nineteenth-century America. The play — not the Doris Day version — has now had several productions, beginning in New York, later adapted into *Calamity Jane — the musical*. Both versions continue to be produced throughout

America. Here I used a biographical play to explore the theme of myth and reality of the Old West. What fascinated me was the wide discrepancy between what really happened and the folk tales and dime novels about figures of the Wild West, like Calamity Jane who was an extraordinary woman far ahead of her time, but suffered from abandonment by Wild Bill Hickok and the challenges of alcoholism. Abandoned and left to raise a child alone and work in a man's world, this story seemed pertinent to life as a woman today.

Sometimes story ideas may arise from what happens to us in our own lives. Yet, even if they don't, they usually connect with something felt within. My first long play was about Virginia Woolf. I was still acting then and had been cast to play Virginia Woolf in the comedy, *An Evening in Bloomsbury* by Victoria Sullivan, produced off-Broadway in New York. Naturally I began reading everything I could find by and about Woolf in order to better portray the character. Long after the play closed, however, I was still reading about her. Then one day I just sat down and started writing a drama about her struggle with madness in a world gone mad, i.e. World War II — a story far removed from the life of this baby boomer raised in New Orleans and Texas. (Remember? Not what you know but what you feel strongly about.) I had long been fascinated by the razor's edge between creative genius and madness: van Gogh, Nijinsky, and Virginia Woolf, to name a few. So this was the theme I chose to explore through her life. *Virginia* (later titled *On the Edge*) had the good fortune to be directed by the legendary Harold Clurman (who launched the plays of Eugene O'Neill and Tennessee Williams). The play went on to win the National Endowment for the Arts Award, but the real reward was the emotional response from the audience. Here's one example. After one evening's performance, an older woman, born in Europe, approached me and was crying. She expressed how grateful she was that I had written of the Kristallnacht incident in my play. Tears filled her eyes as she held my hand tightly, and said simply, "I was there. I was there."

A surprise came when friends would come up after a performance of the play and remark how it reminded them of me.

"It's so you," they would say. I was puzzled. Wasn't this a play about novelist Virginia Woolf? Then slowly I realized that though the facts of the story were quite removed from my own life, the emotional content was in some ways parallel. In other words, the story dealt with themes I felt strongly about — something friends would notice, even if the playwright did not!

Incidentally, this emotional identification with what you write applies to all genres, both fiction and nonfiction. Sometimes it is easier to express yourself in a story far removed in fact from ourselves. Sounds odd, right? Yet sometimes a character far removed from you in time or even gender can be more like you than a character expressly modeled on yourself. For one thing, the characters in a fictional or biographical story tend to be more three-dimensional because the author has the necessary distance in writing them. Have you ever tried to see all sides of yourself? Yet, even when writing about well-known historical figures like Calamity Jane or Virginia Woolf, I still had to make their journey my own, re-discovering the story through myself.

> A truly personal search begins when one realizes that to make the process real, one has no choice but to enter into its rediscovery, step by step, accepting nothing as true until it has become true in one's own experience. One must start from zero, clear an empty space in oneself, and walk the entire journey of the very first searcher who paved the way.
> — Peter Brook, *Threads of Time*

I first met English director Peter Brook at his Le Bouffe du Nord Theatre in Paris where he invited me for lunch and to sit in on a rehearsal of *Carmen*. He wanted to discuss India where I had lived for some years studying Hindu philosophy, for his next theatre project was to be an adaptation of the great Hindu epic, *Mahabharata*. Here was a man touched by a quest, who had courageously broken away from traditional theatre when he was already at the top of his field in England. Brook studied the teachings of Gurdjieff, the Russian-Armenian mystic philosopher (1866-1949), becoming more and more dissatisfied with the emptiness of commercial theatre. He procured an abandoned warehouse in an unfashionable section of Paris and literally created the empty space for a new theatre. So when he produced the well-known story of Carmen, he made it his own by investing in it his vision, values, and feelings. Later on, he did the same with the *Mahabharata*.

Whether you create an original story or re-create a known one, you still must make it your own. And this requires a personal journey, both inner and outer. The outer journey of research and craft is merely the starting point. The best adaptations are never literal. Find the vision of your story from within, and it will guide you to the end. Invisible helpers will appear to light the way.

Sometimes a story might appear in a dream, as did the Disney family film that I wrote for Dolly Parton, *Unlikely Angel*. The theme of unconditional love necessary for spiritual growth, told in a simple way, combined a specific, personal value with a universal truth which found a response in the collective. Often the best ideas arise from our own unconscious minds, either waking or in sleep.

One idea for a play came about in the following way. I was walking down Park Avenue in New York when I saw the *New York Post* headline at a newsstand: "Mother Hurls Baby and Self from Twelfth Story Brownstone." In a flash, I knew my next play. I didn't even bother to read the news story but just adopted the premise. I had wanted to write about something I felt strongly about, that is, the superwoman of the eighties who is pushed over the edge. I had not yet found my story, only what I wanted to say.

Women, like myself, who married young, had children, careers — and wanted to do everything perfectly — often faced an inevitable crisis of overwhelm. This tragic news story headline gave me the starting point for a fictional story that could happen to anyone, when pushed to the extreme. What would happen if a superwoman of the eighties, driven to be perfect as wife, mother, and careerist, was pushed over the edge and did something tragic?

Sometimes to make a story work, you must go to extremes. This is why many successful stories involve a murder or catastrophe. Please understand that I am not referring to gratuitous violence here. Just follow the integrity of your story and go to the end of it. The Swedish screenwriter-director, Ingmar Bergman, is a master of pushing a story to its edge. Where most writers would end their story at a certain point, a genius like Bergman begins with the extreme, then pushes the dramatic action even further. This pushing can result in stories of substance and depth, but demands of the writer to write from his heart and guts as well as his mind. *The Seventh Seal*, *Wild Strawberries*, *Scenes from a Marriage*, and *Saraband* are four examples of Bergman's masterpieces.

The challenge is to discover the meaning for your self in the story you have chosen, and then adopt the necessary form that can be meaningful to others. One might say, first, the passion, and only second is craft necessary to birth an authentic and great story. It is passion in a relationship or marriage that will sustain it for years through thick and thin. Similarly, it is passion in a story that will sustain the writing process through the weeks, months, and sometimes years of completing the work.

How to choose your story then? Simple. Choose the one you feel emotionally connected with.

> What does the brain matter compared with the heart?
> — Virginia Woolf, *Mrs.Dalloway*

Never underestimate the power of a great story. Bill Moyers once interviewed producer David Putnam on NPR Radio. Putnam produced Oscar winner *Chariots of Fire* and *The Mission*, among other fine films. Putnam remarked that "If movies were what they might be, there'd be no need to go to church." Such is the mighty impact of story.

My early play, *Somewhere-in-Between*, produced off-Broadway in New York City in the early seventies, is set in a mental institution. One of the six main characters, Sam, is really sane but keeps finding a way to return to the institution. That is, he feigns insanity in order to escape the outer world. Sam confides to the inmates that the outer world is more insane than the mental ward. Sam becomes a bridge "somewhere-in-between" the two worlds.

Jungian analyst Linda Leonard is aware of how we have forgotten to honor our visionaries:

> In our culture we have lost our awareness of the importance of oracular knowledge, and we fail to honor or even listen to the Visionaries who mediate visions. We have forgotten to revere

the ancient mysteries; we have discarded the rituals that allows the mysteries to unfold and be revealed. In ancient times, the role of priestess (or shaman) was central to human life.

In the film *Wolfbride*, written for the Finnish Film Foundation in the early nineties, I tell the story of Aalo, a Finnish woman living in the seventeenth century who is a healer. She is marked from birth as a wolfbride and called by the Big One, the great wolf. Aalo, too, is a shape changer, that is, both wolf and human. When Valber, Aalo's woman servant, draws symbols in the ashes, Aalo asks her what they mean. Valber replies, "It is the divine couple. It represents the divided soul. Dark and light." Later, here is how Aalo is carried away by the calling of the Big One:

The wolf couple face each other. Aalo looks at the Big One's eyes and loses herself. She realizes he is more than a mere wolf and is the Dark One himself. His form seems to grow large and shimmer in the moonlight and his eyes shine like two red piercing embers. They approach each other, sniffing.

SOUND of wind through the branches as they leap toward each other and roll upon the ground.

CLOSE on their paws as they transform into human hands.

CAMERA widens to see a naked Aalo with a naked STRANGER rolling on the ground in fierce passion. CLOSE on golden resin slowly oozing from the trunk of a tall pine tree. One drop becomes merged into a second drop. Two naked bodies lie intertwined.

He rises and leaves. Aalo awakes and sits up, watching the Stranger, now in wolf form, gallop away.

Aalo has surrendered to her instinctive self, yet returns to her mortal husband in the village. The villagers, driven by fear and superstition, form an angry mob, then burn her to death. Between 1575 and 1700 in Europe, with the blessings of the Church, over one million women were victims of witch hunts. The cost of splitting ourselves between spirit and matter is costly indeed.

The film story of *Wolfbride* describes the danger of this split between matter and spirit. Spirit here does not refer to organized religion, often more invested in the power of the institution than the transformational role of spirit. In her remarkable book, *Shaman*, Joan Halifax writes, "Through creative expression, the human condition is elevated, mythologized, and at last, collectively understood."

How can you write in such a way as to become a bridge between earth and spirit? How can you heal the split in today's fractured society? The healing transformation of good writing depends on making it one's own from within. In other words, what you write is not separate from your deepest self. These are the stories sorely needed today.

Before going further, however, I wish to add a disclaimer. In discussing the craft of writing which I know to be absolutely necessary — even though not everything — I will be laying down rules of story structure and the like in the upcoming chapters. These rules have proved helpful to me and to my students and clients over the years. However — and this is the point — where there are rules, there will be exceptions. Beckettesque Oscar winner *Lost in Translation,* about two lost souls who meet in a Tokyo four-star hotel, is such an exception.

Creativity knows no boundaries. The seed of your story may come to you in different ways. For instance, playwright Arthur Miller usually begins with a theme, as did Henrik Ibsen. Hence, Miller's plays are strongly thematic (*All My Sons*, *Death of a Salesman,* or *The Crucible*). Tennessee Williams, on the other hand, usually begins with a character — for example, Amanda in *A Glass Menagerie*, his most autobiographical play. English playwright Tom Stoppard (*Jumpers*, *Invention of Love*) begins with dialogue he hears in his head. To another writer, sometimes the plot may appear whole — then the writer must add the characters and theme. It matters little where you start, as long as you get where you're going. So there is little point in trying to fit the writing process into some neat formula. There is none. Read this book and others, learn whatever you can, but, in the end, you must find your own way home.

There is never one single road to Rome. Imagine someone pitching the film, *My Dinner with Andre*, at a studio today. The story? Well, these two intellectuals have dinner in New York City. What happens? Well, they just sit at this restaurant and talk and talk and talk. Had *My Dinner with Andre* not been an independently produced film, I doubt it would have ever been made. The result is glorious, as many exceptions are. Never forget that to write experientially, not cerebrally, is the way of story. You may never know where your story will lead. Yet, if you feel passionately about a story, follow it, and it will take you home. Then, if you work hard enough and the gods smile, you may experience the deep pleasure of reading your own work as if for the first time, wondering where it came from!

> Imagination is more important than knowledge.
> — Albert Einstein

Inventor George Washington Carver, born a slave and later becoming one of the great chemists of American history, discovered multiple hitherto unknown uses for the common peanut. His words tell us, "Whatever you love opens its secrets to you." So find what you love.

As an actress and playwright, my passion was for strong character-driven dramas. My first film, *The Christmas Wife*, starring Jason Robards and Julie Harris, proved an exception to the current Hollywood success formula of sex and violence. No car chases or special effects tempted this writer, only what might take place in an intimate room between two lonely people. Well-meaning friends advised that a simple story of two senior citizens who spend the weekend together, without sex or violence, could never be sold as a Hollywood movie. Fate intervened. It is my belief and personal experience that whenever you follow that inner guide, the world will respond, often magically.

I had just written *The Christmas Wife* when I was invited to fly to Hollywood to receive the Julie Harris Award for my Texas play, *The Women of Cedar Creek*. The award was sponsored by the Beverly Hills Theatre Guild, and Ms. Harris — whom I had never before met — would be presenting the award to me at a posh banquet in Beverly Hills. So I packed the new screenplay and flew to Hollywood. At the ceremony, I met the legendary Julie Harris and mentioned that I had just written my first screenplay, and that she would be perfect in the title role. Might she read it? (I just happened to have a copy of the script in my car!) She read the script that very evening and called me the next morning to say that she would love to do it. I had been in Hollywood for twenty-four hours and the only person I knew was Julie Harris.

The next day I flew back to New York and attended a revival of Eugene O'Neill's *The Iceman Cometh* on Broadway starring Jason Robards. I had met Jason in the course of my acting days, so, script in hand, I went backstage to greet him and hand him the script. Within a week, Jason called and said that he would love to do the role, and to work with Miss Harris. A few months later, we were filming in Toronto. And, as I had cast the movie, I was given credit as co-producer. In a short time, I was now a produced screenwriter and a producer.

Truly, a Cinderella story of launching a career in Hollywood. The HBO film went on to be nominated for the Cable Ace Awards for Best Movie, Best Writing, Best Actor, and Best Actress. It received over two hundred unanimous rave reviews, confirming to me that people do want something different — even on television! All I did was follow the themes I felt strongly about: loneliness and how it is never possible to recreate the past. That's all I did ... besides sitting down and writing the story, of course.

The hardest part is sitting down. I write this on the board the first day of every class. And then add that there is no guarantee that you will write a great story, book, play or screenplay. But one thing is certain. As Shakespeare's *King Lear* says, "Nothing will come of nothing." You can never write a great story until you sit down and write *a* story. And this takes a certain amount of courage. In my own experience, I have learned that courage is needed whether writing your very first effort or your fiftieth! Writing is not about overcoming fear, but keeping on in spite of the fear! In fact, fear provides tension, essential in any creative process. So trust the fear. It means you're in the mix.

The first purpose of writing is to clarify and reveal something in yourself, but the only way to do this is to get it out of yourself. The second purpose of writing is to share it with others, providing a mirror for humanity at large, as a modern day shaman.

First, you must discover meaning for yourself in the story you have chosen and then find the necessary form that can be meaningful for others. Notice, too, that every story you write will be a totally different experience, both in origin and in process. This is why I am dead set against any pat formulas for writing anything. Just create the space within and listen to your story. It will guide you. One story might be served best as a short story or a novel, another as a play or film. Remember though, passion first, then craft. The essence of Art is to use the outer form to convey an inner experience. This sacred thread, your innermost being or Soul, binds you emotionally to what you write, and if given respect, will lead you on to the desired end. Stories written from this center will move mountains — and even create livelihoods. Years ago, when interviewed by the *New York Times* about my approach to teaching, I was quoted as saying, "We've become lopsided living only in our heads. Writing, in order to serve the soul, must integrate outer craft with the inner world of intuition and feeling."

Here's a visualization exercise that can begin to tap hidden resources. And never forget that your most valuable resource is yourself. If you are a professional writer already, I ask you to do the following exercises as though you have never written anything before today. Approach the blank page as if for the first time. You might choose to play some sacred or soothing music as you do the following exercise. This exercise serves as an invocation and ritual to summon the Muse.

EXERCISE: SOUL DIALOGUE

Close your eyes. Trust the space made sacred by our intention. Now take three deep breaths. Inhale and exhale. As you exhale, take the thought "I release all fear of this inner journey." Repeat this thought on the next two exhalations. Breathe in ... breathe out. "I release all fear of this inner journey. " And so, the journey begins.

I'd like you to visualize a long path which stretches before you. It may be a place known to you or it may be a new terrain. It may pass through a dark wood or across high mountains. At some point, you see before you an ancient iron gate. The gate is locked and vines cover it. You reach deep into your pocket and find a key. The key is large and rather heavy. Place the key into the lock, turning it in a complete circle so that the gate swings open. Now take another deep breath, releasing any residue of fear, and walk through the open gate.

You find yourself now in a garden. It might be an English garden or perhaps a Japanese Zen garden with stone lanterns and tranquil pools of water with white lotus and gentle koi fish. Or any garden of your choice. See it. The flowers are in bloom. The smells intoxicate, causing you to smile. Just ahead lies a house which you recognize as the house of your dreams. You know this house for it is your very Self. Take a moment and visualize your house.

The door is locked but you hold in your hand the key. Visualize the key to your house and, taking a deep breath, open the door. Enter now and stand for a moment, taking in the profound feeling that you have come Home. Then slowly yet with purpose, walk to your favorite room. Perhaps a paneled study lined with books of favorite authors. A fireplace glows providing warmth. Now walk to a large desk which overlooks the garden, and sit. After a moment, open the center drawer and take out paper and pen. See the pen that you will write with. Now look carefully at the virgin white page and honor it. Soon it will be time to write your first Soul Dialogue.

But first, I'd like you to visualize your Soul. It might be a bird or a butterfly or an animal. Or a jewel or some other precious object. What would be a metaphor for your Soul, your innermost being? See it. Experience it.

Now begin the dialogue. Visualize looking at your Soul in whatever form it has chosen. Then ask it, your Soul, this simple question: What do you want?

This will not be the only or final answer for all time, simply the one Soul gives you today, that is now, this very moment.

For the next five minutes — without undue thinking — open your eyes and begin the exercise, the Soul dialogue. Simply write the question, "What do you want?" Then taking all the time you need, listen for Soul's reply and write it down. Write it all down. There is no right answer. There is only your answer. Please begin now.

EXERCISE: THE EMPTY SCREEN

Take a blank piece of paper and draw a large rectangle on the page. It should look like a blank movie screen before the movie starts. Place this on the wall near where you write.

Now simply watch the blank screen and see what images and story appear. Use very little effort here — just passively observe what comes up from your own unconscious mind. It may be no more than a passing image — say a white gull dipping over an ocean. Follow the bird. See what unfolds.

EXERCISE: WHAT IF . . .

Write the words "what if" followed by one or two sentences. This is the premise of a story. An example: What if a young man finds out who his father really is. Write three separate *what if* premises for three possible story situations.

Anyone is capable of finding a story. The plain fact is not everyone will invest the time and passion to write it down. A writer is one who writes, so make writing a priority for at least part of each day.

In the next few chapters, I will focus on the craft of story. Though craft is, of course, necessary in creating a good story, please remember that it is only a tool allowing the writer to give expression to something much deeper, something uniquely his. Craft, in order to serve the vision, will become the bridge between earth and spirit so urgently needed today.

As Amagatzu, the founder of the innovative Japanese dance-drama called Butoh, once said:

> The Soul is the important thing.
> Form will follow.

The aim of Butoh is to reach the essence of feeling. That is your aim, too.

Chapter 2

Seven Steps to Story Structure

The three most vital elements in any good film are the script, the script, the script.
— Alfred Hitchcock

*J*EAN PAUL SARTRE once said that the freedom of Bach's musical genius came from his tremendous discipline and technique. It is the same with good writing. Even though writing comes from within and the work begins there, as we have explored in chapter one, craft is essential. Many wonderful and inspired story ideas may have the short life of a mayfly. Monet, the impressionist painter, once remarked to his friend, the great poet, Mallarme, "I have many ideas for poems, but somehow they never seem to come out quite right." Whereupon, Mallarme quipped, "That is because poetry is not written with ideas, but with words!"

The handicap under which most beginning writers struggle is that they don't know how to write. I was no exception to this rule.
— P. G. Wodehouse

Story must be captured by craft. It is only through craft and discipline that you can achieve the pure freedom of creative expression. In terms of the craft of writing, three things matter: structure, structure, and structure!

In Hollywood, there is a lot of mystique and frenzy over story structure: what it is, how to nail the structure of the story, and so on. What is story structure then? Simply put, the order of your scenes — that is, the order of what your main character does. Remember Aristotle: Plot is character. It is the order of your story that becomes the structure. Professionals work from structure to dialogue and not the other way round. So, simply put, story structure is the sequence of scenes.

Before writing my first film, *The Christmas Wife*, I used index cards to designate each individual scene: which characters are present and what is the purpose of the scene in one or two sentences. Then I could easily re-arrange the order of scenes at will. This proved helpful when I was learning the craft of screenwriting where story structure is so important. I have noticed with students, for instance, that beginning writers often make the mistake of revealing too much too soon. It's a little like meeting someone at a party — the less they say about themselves, the more interesting they seem. Or the other way round. As the old vaudevillians knew, always leave them asking for more. Using the index cards, you might move some exposition in scene two to the second act, thereby heightening the mystery of both character and plot. In *Casablanca* — the little B-movie that became a classic — the lovers' past unravels a little bit at a time, heightening the mystery of what actually happened in Paris between Bogart and Bergman. Not knowing the whole story keeps the audience attentive, wanting more.

"The basis of a novel is a story, and a story is a narrative of events arranged in a time sequence," says E. M. Forster, author of *Howard's End* and *A Room with a View*.

I can't resist sharing an anecdote about once meeting E. M. Forster. I was on my honeymoon in England with my husband, the Indian novelist Raja Rao. We were invited for tea by Mr. Forster at his bachelor digs at Kings College, Cambridge. What I remember most was Forster's bare modesty and elegant simplicity as he prepared tea for us on a gas burner in his rooms. As we sat together, he said that many had asked him why he stopped writing after publishing only a few novels, and he had told them, "It's very simple, really. I had nothing more to say. " It was only later that same year when, having read all five of his novels, that I realized this modest gentleman had written a veritable masterpiece, *Howard's End*. Here was one who had mastered the craft of writing story.

Forster remarked once, "Plot reveals human intentions. A plot is a narrative of events. The king died and then the queen died is a story. The king died and the queen died of grief is a plot. A story answers what happened next; a plot tells us why. " The why of what happens is connected with character and character motivations. It is impossible to separate plot from character. Aristotle was right.

Joseph Campbell, the mythologist, was an amazing man. I met him and his wife, Jean Erdman, in New York, and had the great fortune to spend time with them. He wrote of the hero's journey in *The Hero with a Thousand Faces*. Campbell outlined the structure of myth in this way: The opening stage includes the call to adventure, meeting the mentor, and the journey. Once into the adventure, the challenges involve: finding allies and guides, facing ordeals, resisting temptations, braving enemies, enduring the dark night of the soul, surviving the supreme ordeal, and achieving the goal. The concluding steps are: the return journey, resurrection, celebration, accepting a role of service, and, finally, merging two worlds.

George Lucas pays tribute to Campbell's hero's journey as a great influence when he wrote the *Star Wars* films. Many writers could do worse than adopt the myth structure as a model for creating their stories. It will lift an ordinary story and give it mythic, universal qualities.

Before I talk about the Seven Steps to Story Structure, it might be a good idea to focus on what should be included in the early part of your story. Again, remember that what applies to screenwriting is also helpful in writing other narrative forms. In screenwriting, for instance, within the first ten to twenty minutes of the screenplay or film, the following should be revealed:

- The setting: time and place of the story
- Genre of story: drama, comedy, mystery, etc.
- Introduction of main character or main characters.

- Inciting incident
- The problem of the story.

There is nothing more frustrating than to begin reading a novel or viewing a film and discover half an hour later that the genre promised at the opening of the story is not the one the novel or film delivers. Another example might be watching what is purported to be a serious drama and discovering much later that it is actually a farce. There are of course legitimate mixed genres, such as comedy-dramas like *Terms of Endearment* or mystery-comedies like *Gosford Park*. But whatever the genre, just be straight with your reader or audience from the start. You don't want to alienate them. Never betray your audience. Once you've lost them, it's difficult to entice them back.

It is also distracting if you cannot orient yourself as to where and when the story takes place. If watching a film that has not disclosed setting, I keep looking at car license plates to find a clue to where I am, and cannot settle and open to the story until such exposition is resolved. Of course, once in a while, there will be a notable exception to this rule, as in Samuel Beckett's existentialist play, *Waiting for Godot*, where it serves the story for the audience to be as lost as the characters are. Generally, however, it is best to provide the necessary exposition of where, when, how, and what.

Every story in any genre must have a problem. For example, *Dr. Zhivago* by Pasternak is set in early twentieth-century Russia just before and during the Russian revolution. Yuri, the hero of the novel, is torn between an aristocratic life of beauty, love, and poetry — and the Revolution. He is also torn between a conventional marriage and a mistress he loves. Life versus the destruction of life is the ongoing theme of this great novel and film.

A few years ago I wrote an original story for Disney Studios which became a film starring Dolly Parton titled *Unlikely Angel*. The story is about a country western singer (Who) who dies and goes to heaven (Where). However, she is having trouble earning her wings because she is still too attached to earth and earthly pleasures (Problem). She is assigned by St. Peter (Who) to return to earth on a mission, her last chance before being sent below to the other place (Genre: romantic comedy). The mission is this: She must return to earth and be a nanny to a troubled family. If she succeeds in helping them before Christmas, she will be allowed to remain in Heaven, earning her wings at last.

Another valuable tool, structurally, is the *ticking clock*. This ups the ante, intensifying the action of your story. In *Unlikely Angel*, the ticking clock is that Dolly has only two weeks before Christmas for her mission to be accomplished or she goes to hell. In the Oscar-winning script *Sideways*, it is a few days before the wedding. *High Noon* is another of many examples, along with virtually everything directed by Alfred Hitchcock. Please note that all stories benefit from the ticking clock, not only those in the mystery or thriller genre.

So, in the first 11 minutes of the Disney family film cited above, the setting is introduced (that is, the world of the story), the genre (romantic comedy), the main characters (Dolly, St. Peter, and the family), and the problem. These join together to launch the inciting incident or first major beat of the story. This is when Dolly suddenly drops down to earth, landing plop in front of the motherless family's home (Where). Lift off. The ride has begun!

Perhaps I should say more about the *inciting incident*. Stories today, as films, must offer an inciting incident within ten to twenty minutes of the opening. This means that the setting, genre, main characters, and problem have been clearly introduced. The inciting incident is akin to sitting in a roller coaster, then suddenly experiencing that first jolt or movement. In the Oscar-winning screenplay and film, *Witness*, it's the moment the young Amish boy, played by Lukas Haas, witnesses the murder. The car crash at the beginning of the Oscar winner *Crash* is another example. We know what kind of story it is and what the problem is. The ride has begun!

The inciting incident is the first *beat* of your story. A beat is a dramatic moment which either enhances character or advances plot. I first learned of beats while studying acting in New York with Broadway actress, Uta Hagen, who was also a fine teacher. I highly recommend her book, *Respect for Acting*, for writers as well as actors, as it is a great tool for developing both character and story beats.

The first scene I did in Hagen's class was a scene from *Hamlet* where I played Ophelia. I had already studied and been directed by B. Iden Payne, once director of Stratford-on-Avon, England, so I felt confident of my Shakespearean style. Of course, Hagen mercilessly tore me to shreds, saying "I want you to play an Ophelia I believe goes to the bathroom!" After recovering from initial shock and my regional actor's pride, I realized that I had much to learn. My abstractly romantic Ophelia did not walk on this earth. Lesson: Characters must be three-dimensional, grounded, and not just an extension of the writer's projected aesthetic imagination.

I also encourage students and clients to enroll in an improvisational acting class, especially for dramatic writing such as plays and screenplays. It is important to experience that dialogue and action in a play or film must be in the present, spontaneously happening now, unlike a novel which might be introspective or taking place in the past. Improvisation is a valuable tool for learning this.

In New York, I acted for a year and a half in an improvisational troupe which played off-Broadway in Greenwich Village. We performed for live audiences and never knew exactly what we might say or do. It was spontaneous and fun. I still regard this as the best acting class I ever had, as well as a superb prep for playwriting and screenwriting. Why? Because when you have to think on your feet in the midst of a situation with another person, what you say must come directly from you. There is no time to rationalize or try and remember what to say, it is happening *now*. And now is when all good plays and screenplays take place.

The *Way of Story* approach to writing includes the whole of you, not just the rational mind. You must bring all of you to the table: body and guts, feelings, intuition — yes, even your dreams. A writer must make use of all his resources, and they are blessedly manifold as we shall explore in the upcoming chapters.

The following steps, inspired by a talk by John Truby, should help clarify your story's structure. After first listing the following steps, I will later illustrate with examples.

THE SEVEN STEPS TO STORY STRUCTURE

1. **Problem/Need of main character**: He will be very aware of the problem but not how to solve it. Need is inside, often hidden. Something is missing in the main character or protagonist which is usually based on a character flaw.

2. **Desire: A particular goal.** Here it is important to distinguish between Need and Desire. A lion is hungry; this is his need. Then he sees a gazelle running: the gazelle is the specific desire. To fulfill his need, he must obtain his desire. Though need and desire are linked, they are not the same thing.

3. **Opponent**: Competing for the same or opposite goal and/ or same territory. There may be both external and internal opponents.

4. **The Plan**: A set of guidelines the hero/heroine or protagonist uses to overcome the opponent or antagonist and reach his goal, obtaining his specific desire. Things inevitably go wrong, and the hero has to re-group, finding new solutions. There will be many milestones before the final battle.

5. **Final Battle**: The conflicts get more and more intense. The Final Battle is the last conflict.

6. **Self-Revelation**: The lies are stripped away. The hero undergoes a profound change where he learns something fundamental about who he is, and his place in the world. The best stories will also have a moral revelation. That is, not just who he is but how he should act with others.

7. **A New Life begins**: The hero is either at a higher or lower level than at the beginning of the story. This may be either positive or negative. A test question might be: how has my main character changed in some fundamental way?

(Please note that Steps 5-7 most often take place in the last ten minutes of a film story.)

Now, let us examine each step using David Mamet's 1982 Oscar-winning screenplay adaptation of *The Verdict*, a novel by Barry Reed, to illustrate. *The Verdict* is an excellent example of a well-structured story.

1. **Problem/Need of main character**: *The Verdict* opens with Frank Galvin (Paul Newman), an alcoholic lawyer in Boston,

who is dropping by funeral homes to get work from bereaved widows. Here is a man obviously at the bottom of the barrel. At first glance, you might say that Frank's need is to stop drinking, but the need is usually deeper than the surface or first look. Later on it is revealed that Frank Galvin was once an idealistic lawyer who believed in justice and was at the top of his profession. He lost his faith in justice during a corrupt case where bribes won the day. When he confronted his boss and tried to do the right thing, he was stripped of everything: job and marriage. So his *need* is to believe in justice again. Alcoholism is merely the symptom of the underlying problem or need.

2. **Desire** is always a particular goal, never general. Remember the hungry lion and the running gazelle. Frank Galvin is given the case of a young girl who due to medical negligence in a Catholic hospital is now a vegetable for life. Frank Galvin wants to win this case, that's his specific desire. His need is to believe in justice again. This is why he surprises himself by turning down the generous settlement offer from the Catholic Church and insists on going to trial. Sometimes the need is unconscious, unknown even to the hero. The desire, on the other hand, will always be conscious and specific.

3. **Opponent** will be competing for the same goal or territory. In *The Verdict*, Frank is fighting the institution of the Catholic Church that owns the hospital where medical negligence has been done to his client. Specifically, the opponent is a villainous attorney, portrayed by James Mason, who combats Frank both in and out of the courtroom. It is a David and Goliath story, long popular in Hollywood films, and a familiar American myth where the little guy takes on the mighty corporation or power and wins the day. (*Erin Brockovich* with Julia Roberts, Elijah Wood as Frodo in *The Lord of the Rings,* or Gary Cooper in *High Noon* are three examples.)

4. **The Plan**: A set of guidelines the hero uses to overcome the opponent and reach the goal. Things inevitably go wrong, and new solutions must be found. Frank has Dr. Gruber, an expert witness, to testify, but the powerful defense attorney (James Mason) representing the Catholic Church gets to him first. Dr. Gruber has now left the country, and the Judge, also bought by the Church, refuses

to grant an extension. Even Frank's mistress (Charlotte Rampling) is discovered to be on the payroll of the opposing side, as an informer. One by one, Frank's case is crucified. It appears all is lost, with no where to turn, and then…

5. **The Final Battle** provides the final conflict: It's never over until it's over. The day before the end of the trial, Frank discovers a missing witness and flies to New York to convince her to testify. She does and wins the day. David has killed Goliath.

6. **Self-Revelation**. Here, as in the best of stories, there is a moral revelation: Justice for the poor and downtrodden against the mighty power machines. Doing the right thing.

7. **A New Life Begins**. Frank Galvin wins the case against insurmountable odds, and with it, re-discovers his belief in justice, and is thereby transformed. Though his specific desire is to win the case, his real need is to believe in justice again, and, consequently, in himself. Now a new life begins, full of hope and promise.

Also here, as in the best of stories, there is a moral revelation: justice for the poor and downtrodden against the mighty power machines. Doing the right thing.

It was said earlier that Step 7: A New Life, might be either positive or negative. A negative example would be the Billy Wilder classic, *Sunset Boulevard*, when fading screen star Norma Desmond discovers she's been living a lie and goes mad, killing the messenger played by William Holden.

Let's take another example, the 1999 Oscar-nominated screenplay and film by M. Night Shyamalan, *The Sixth Sense*.

1. **Problem/Need**: Bruce Willis, a noted child psychologist, once failed with a young boy who grows up to be a psychotic killer, seen in the bathroom scene at the beginning of the movie. So his need is to redeem himself from this failure and not fail again.

2. **Desire**: To succeed with his current patient, the young boy played by Haley Joel Osment (nominated for an Oscar as Best Supporting Actor).

3. **Opponent**: Here the opponent is really fear, both inner and outer: the boy's fear to reveal himself as one who sees dead people, and the psychologist's acceptance that he is one as well.

4. **The Plan**: To overcome the fear by confronting the ghosts the boy sees.

5. **The Final Battle**: The B-story of the young girl who has been killed.

6. **Self-Revelation**: The lies have been stripped away. Willis realizes that he himself is dead, and a ghost himself.

7. **A New Life**: Willis must let go of his earthly life, releasing his wife, and move on.

Incidentally, one can draw on some of the structure points above as a guide to making each separate scene in your story work. Simply use the seven steps as a check list for each scene.

Another tool focuses on structuring each scene by adapting the following five points:

Five Points in Making a Good Scene

1. *Character's intention*: What does he want and why? In *Witness*, Harrison Ford's specific desire is to protect the witness and find the killer. His need, however is to love and to expand his world view via the Amish widow played by Kelly McGillis.

2. *Desire* is what drives scene and story, but it is the need that gives your story its depth.

3. *Opponent:* Who wants to stop this character getting what he wants and why.

4. *The Plan*: Determine the plan of each scene from your main character's viewpoint. For instance, the hero says, "I want" and the opponent says, "No".

An indirect plan might be where your text becomes subtext. That is, the main character of a scene says one thing while really meaning something else.

5. *Overall pacing*: Conflict of action (what the main character is doing) and conflict of being (who the character is). For instance, in *Witness,* the soft love scenes are contrasted with the fast action crime scenes.

"I try to be conscious about the rhythms of storytelling."
— Michael Mann (director of *Traffic*)

It is a good idea to contrast your scenes after writing your first draft. Alternate the types of scenes. (Sometimes screenwriters use index cards for this purpose as earlier described. Each card will have a sentence or two describing the scene.) To alternate scenes, for instance, have a fast-paced action scene follow a quiet scene, an indoor scene follow one outdoors, noisy follow quiet, dark scene follow a light scene, and so on.

SET UPS AND PAY OFFS

One of the best ways to create a powerful emotional response in your reader and audience is to utilize Set Ups and Pay Offs. Casually introduce something at the beginning of your story, the significance of which is only later — usually at the end — understood. Anton Chekhov once said, "If you introduce a gun in Act I, it has to go off in Act III" as shown in his play, *The Seagull.*

The set up can be a metaphor which reveals theme as in *Citizen Kane* where the young boy is brutally taken from his home while playing with his sled named Rosebud. At the end of his life, though now wealthy, his last word is "Rosebud." Though the world is puzzled as to its meaning, the audience knows that Rosebud symbolizes a lost childhood, a home he was never to find again.

It can also be a major plot device as in *Sixth Sense* where in the first five minutes of the film we see an intruder fire a shot at Bruce Willis before killing himself. It's only at the very end of the film that we realize the consequences of the opening event. This is an "aha!" experience, and quite powerful.

Recently I was invited by the Santa Barbara Women's Club to a screening of my film, *The Christmas Wife*, which came out several years back. It was confirming to hear, as several of the two hundred women and men approached me, how surprised and moved they were by the ending of the film. Here, too, is an example of set up and pay off. The early scene in the escort service office appears insignificant until the final moments of the film where it provides a startling discovery.

Both *Presumed Innocent* by novelist Scott Turow, later a film starring Harrison Ford, and *LA Confidential* have powerful endings thanks to well executed set ups and pay offs. In both these films, the clues to who did it are everywhere, though you can't quite put it together until the end. Both writers here earned their pay off.

If pay offs are not well executed, they become cheap devices: plot devices which appear from nowhere, leaving the audience with a feeling not of "aha" but of being cheated, manipulated. For the pay offs to work, the set ups must be clearly, if discreetly, there. When honestly done, they are worth their weight in gold because of the emotional power they bring.

When I started writing feature films in Hollywood for major studios, I began to learn the three-act structure. Movies seen in the theatres are generally written with an Act I, Act 2, and Act 3 format.

Here is the breakdown in pages for a feature screenplay, usually about one and a half to two hours:

Act 1: pages 1-30
Act 2: pages 30-90
Act 3: pages 90-120

Later on, I discovered that this was also helpful in early drafts of movies for network television — even though television movies are written in seven acts.

A teleplay for a two-hour television movie will usually be about one hundred and ten pages divided into seven acts, sixteen pages in each act. Why seven acts? Because of the commercial breaks required for television. Once the commercial breaks for television movies were twelve minutes for every two-hour movie — now they are about twenty minutes. This means about twenty minutes of commercials are shown for every two-hour movie.

So, even when writing television movies, I would first write a three-act structured script and only later split it up into the required seven-act structure demanded for television two-hour movies. This is because the three-act structure affords a solid foundation to work from, and, quite simply, you have a better film. I have learned now that the basic three-act structure also serves the play or novel, especially today when media has so influenced plays and novels.

Again, the basic three-act structure for writing a feature screenplay is applicable to all forms of narrative writing. Obviously the page number count given below may differ for other forms of writing narrative. It is interesting to observe that plays were once written in three acts but no longer are. I cannot help but ponder if perhaps we may have lost something when plays became shorter, and de-structured, as it were.

Here again is the basic three-act structure for screenplays with some added guidelines:

Act 1 (pages1-30): Introduction of setting (time and place), genre (type of story), main characters, and the basic problem. The hero knows the problem and what he has to do. Set ups are also laid down here for later pay-offs, i.e., the sled, Rosebud, in *Citizen Kane*.

Act 2 (pages 30-90): Escalating conflicts resulting in the Final Battle at the end of Act 2.

Act 3 (pages 90-110 or 120): Resolution and lesson, preferably a moral lesson of the main character.

Here is a Script Table for those interested in writing for television or film:

Approximate Page Numbers	Running Time	Act Length
30	1/2 -hour teleplay	2 Acts/15 pages
60	1-hour teleplay	4 acts/15 pages
90	90-minute teleplay	6 acts/15 pages
110	2-hour teleplay	7 acts/16 pages
120-150	2-hour feature screenplay	Basic 3-act structure

Here is a further breakdown of Story Structure for the one-hour drama series such as I wrote for the popular television series, *Touched by an Angel*.

Page breakdown for 1-hour drama series for television	
1-3	Cold opening (before credits)
4-18	Act 1
19-31	Act 2
32-46	Act 3
47-56	Act 4
[52-54	Revelation]

If you have ever seen a *Touched by an Angel* episode, you may notice that the revelation at the end of the show — that is, when Della Reese or Roma Downey reveal themselves to be angels and white light surrounds them, will occur precisely at the same time each week, pages 52-54: Revelation. So when I wrote for this show, I had to honor the above table structure precisely. Perhaps this provides a hint as to why television shows sometimes seem so formulaic and predictable. They are meant to be! Television audiences tend to like what is familiar.

A caution is given here. Though structure is important, even very important, please do not forget that story is much more than the sequence of events. It is the inner psychological state of the main character which fuels or drives the external plot.

Here is a humorous example of how structure pays off from a colleague, Frank Daniel, who taught first at Columbia University and then at University of Southern California Film Department in Los Angeles, where I also taught for several years.

Cohen is sitting at the bedside of his wife, who is dying. Suddenly she says to her husband, "Cohen, I must tell you something. " And he says, "Sarah, please. " But she goes on, "No, I must confess. I was unfaithful to you. " "Sarah," he says, "don't get so excited. " She goes on, "But I slept with all your friends and everyone in the town!" Then he says, "Sarah, why do you think I put the poison in your coffee?"

Now, imagine this story told in its time continuity. The audience sees everything and then, as she is dying, she confesses to what we have already seen. Here, it is structure (order of your scenes) that makes the joke or story work. There is a difference between the logic of life and the structure of a good of a good story.

EXERCISE

Take five to ten minutes and make up a story, any story, from your memory or something new that wants to come through. Limit it to one page. Don't rewrite, just do a rough first draft of the story. Now focusing on structure, play around with changing the order of your scenes. For instance, something revealed in the beginning is now shifted to near the end of the story. See how this heightens mystery and adds an exciting twist.

EXERCISE

Re-read your story applying the 7 Steps to Story Structure.

- Problem/Need of main character
- Desire (specific)
- Opponent
- The Plan
- The Final Battle
- Self-Revelation
- A New Life

EXERCISE

Answer the following two questions, using your story. Try to complete each one in one sentence.

    1. This is a story about .... .

    2. The moral dilemma of this story is ...

In the pursuit of any craft, there is much to learn. Discovering more about your story can seem an endless journey, but one well worth the effort.

It is time to approach the Story Outline which takes the journey from the initial vision to the marketplace. In the film *Julia*, Julia (Vanessa Redgrave) turns to playwright Lillian Hellman (Jane Fonda) and says, "Be very bold." Excellent advice for any writer! Read on.

Chapter 3

Writing the Story Outline:

From Vision to Marketplace

I write outlines a lot. Not always scene by scene, but the basic
story points.
— Bruce Joel Rubin (*Ghost, Stuart Little 2*)

As a playwright and short story writer, I never wrote story
outlines. Knowing now all I have learned from writing
screenplays where structure is crucial, I would first write an outline
before writing any narrative form.

Why? There are two reasons: it helps to nail the structure of
the story, and it is an excellent marketing tool. It lets the buyer
know in three to five pages exactly what the story is. Writing the
list of chapters in a book serves roughly the same purpose. So
whether submitting a book proposal to an agent or publisher or
trying to sell a movie idea, writing the story outline helps to move
the writer from vision to the marketplace.

Working in Hollywood gave me the opportunity to learn how
to write story outlines because they are required to pitch or tell
your story to studio or television executives. Remember that in the
beginning storytelling was primarily verbal, oral traditions handed

down from one fireside to another. This tradition is alive and well in Hollywood.

Not many know the origin of the word "pitch" but it might help to understand how important it is. The story goes that during the Spanish Inquisition, Torquemada would tell imprisoned playwrights that if they could interest him in an idea, he would let them live long enough to write it. If not, they were dropped into a large vat of boiling tar, hence the term "pitch." So never underestimate the value of a well-executed pitch!

When I first came to Hollywood as a New York playwright, I was invited to pitch stories to executives. They would ask if I had a story outline to leave with them. You rarely pitch to the person who has the power to green light the project, but to someone lower on the totem pole. They, in turn, go and pitch to their boss. Hence, it helps them — and you — if they have a concise and clear outline to refer to when they in turn tell your story to the powers that be.

In olden days in Hollywood, studio heads such as Louis B. Mayer would say, "Just tell me the story" — not let me read the story. The fact is, most Hollywood execs do not like to read. Jack Warner (Warner Brothers) once said, "I would rather take a fifty-mile hike than crawl through a book." Sam Goldwyn (MGM) remarked, "I read part of it all the way through."

Early on, I actually received a rejection letter from one of the top three talent agencies in Los Angeles which stated, "I read your title page and don't feel it's right for us." Title page means simply the title of the screenplay and my name! (Hollywood is not for the faint of heart!)

No sensible architect would embark on building a house before spending ample time on a blueprint. Writing a story outline provides the necessary blueprint for building story.

Once I served as a writing consultant for a new client's feature screenplay and had to tell him to cut the first forty pages, as his story did not really begin until page forty-one! Had he spent time on his outline, this could easily have been avoided.

Naturally, some things may change when you are in the process of writing your narrative. No outline is written in stone, though it serves as the foundation for your story. By writing and re-writing your outline, the story structure becomes solid. This way when you go to MSS or script, you can save a lot of time and grief in re-writing.

When first asked for an outline by a studio development person, I asked if they had a sample so I would know the correct form to follow. "There's no special form," I was told, so I made up my own. My students and clients have found this a useful sample, but feel free to create your own, if you wish.

LOVE AND DEATH IN TUSCANY

by
Catherine Ann Jones
(based on the novel by Isabelle Holland)

THE SETTING
Italy, the seventies

THE CHARACTERS

PHOEBE, 30s, from Alabama now living in Italy, eccentric free spirit

MEG, 15, her rebellious daughter

COTTON, 30s, artist and friend

PETER SMITH, 40s, English, irresponsible but charming lover of Phoebe, a classical scholar who earns his living by writing porn novels

ALAN GRANT, 40s, Meg's father now an Anglican priest

SYLVIA, 50s, wealthy American who owns a 15th-century castle, outrageous and wonderful

THE THEME

A character-driven drama about love and death. A confrontation between spiritual and human love.

THE STORY

PHOEBE, an extraordinary woman who lives by her
heart and no rules, makes a meager living as a
tour guide in Tuscany. She has just learned that
she will die within six months to a year. Concerned
about her illegitimate daughter, MEG, 15, she
decides to reveal who the father is. She contacts
him and has him come to meet the daughter he never
knew existed until now.

ALAN, now a priest, is troubled by doubts about
his calling which are further challenged when he
reunites with Phoebe — whom he refers to as a
force of nature — and discovers parenthood in his
confrontational relationship with Meg.

MEG is at that awkward stage, trying to discover
who she is. How to react to a father you thought
was dead and who never knew he even had a
daughter? Then when you learn your mother is dying,
anger is easier somehow.

PETER, Phoebe's charming but rather helpless lover
has an alcohol problem and is not a suitable
candidate for fatherhood.

COTTON, gay and a close friend of Phoebe's. Ever
since she can remember, Meg has been in love with
him. She wants to remain with Cotton rather than
her unknown father, which only intensifies the
conflict between her eccentric, unpredictable mother
and herself.

SYLVIA, outrageous, generous, and perceptive, is a
close friend. Five marriages later, Sylvia lives in
a 15th-century castle and surrounds herself with
only interesting people. "Who but Phoebe could teach
us that death is just another part of living?"

As you can see, this outline is only one page in length. It is for a feature screenplay or two-hour television movie. Later I did a fifteen-page treatment of the same project. A one-pager is sometimes useful as it concisely tells your story, and helps you focus the story, as well as serve when trying to market it. It offers a glimpse of what your story is, its style and major theme, as well as introduces your main characters. Just list the major characters, not all. Usually, my outlines are three to five pages in order to further delineate the story beats. Sometimes producers request longer outlines, called film treatments, so there will be no surprises when the script is finally written.

Now let us examine more closely what should be in the story outline, beginning first with the title of your story. A good title should be easy to remember and not too long. It should also provide a good clue to what your story is about. I have seen good films fade away because of a poor title. For instance, a wonderful film which stars Judd Hirsch and Christine Lahti, *Running on Empty* (1988), came and went rather quickly. I think it was because of the title. No one could remember it, even after seeing the film. I heard people say that they saw this great film and wanted to recommend it to their friends — only they couldn't remember the title! Also it is a puzzle as to what kind of story you will be seeing. "Running on Empty" — a racing movie? Many titles refer to the main character, such as *Schindler's List, Thelma and Louise, Lawrence of Arabia, Capote,* and *Driving Miss Daisy. Driving Miss Daisy* not only introduces the main character but also the relationship of the main characters as well as the theme of the story. Not bad in just three words! Another Oscar winner, too.

A good title is important for the writer as well as the marketplace, because it helps the writer to focus the story. Many stories fail because they ramble all over the place, and it's never really clear what the story is or even whose story it is. That is, who are the main character and main characters whose point of view is being explored? If it's your first project, don't try and put five stories into this one. One is quite sufficient.

Next comes the setting of the story. The world of your story is often the hook that draws the reader or audience in, right from the start. In the outline example given above, Italy is the world of the story. So the outline will describe luscious shots of the locale, drawing the audience in. Who wouldn't want a holiday in Tuscany for the price of a movie ticket!

Then the main characters are introduced. The outline should be as concise as possible and written in shorthand, not necessarily in complete sentences. Forget English 101. Simply list your main characters in CAPS then their ages and a few words describing each and the relationship of each to the other main characters. Also CAP the name of your characters when they are first introduced in the script.

The *Story* is where you reveal the significant beats of your story. This should arise from character so that it will be a character-driven story. Not what happens but how and why he does what he does and how his actions transform him and those around him. This carries more weight and is certainly more interesting. This is so because it allows the reader or audience to identify with someone, and in this way, enter the story.

The *Theme* is next. Sometimes you may not know what your story is about until you complete a first draft. If you know already, well and good. The theme is about love and death in *Love and Death in Tuscany*. Theme is different from plot.

Let's revisit a previously given example to distinguish between plot and theme. *Gone with the Wind* is not about the Civil War. The War is merely the backdrop or venue of the love story between Rhett Butler and Scarlett O'Hara. The theme might be: knowing what you want before it's too late. Or, to love not an illusion, but what is real.

As I did in the last paragraph of the sample outline, you might wish to add some dialogue if it reveals character or gives a sense of style. Note Sylvia's line, "Who but Phoebe could teach us that death is just another part of living?" This shows us what kind of character Sylvia is and also reveals the main character, Phoebe, illustrates both theme and story, as does the title, Love and Death in Tuscany. Hence, in a one-page outline, everything is more or less known. Outlines should be as clear and simple as possible as to the genre of the story (drama), problem (Meg's coping with meeting her father for the first time while her mother is dying), and a sense of who the main characters are and their relationships to one another.

Both of the sample outlines are adaptations of another work, usually a novel or book, sometimes a true story, newspaper article, or play. However, the form is the same whether you're writing an original story or adapting someone else's.

A passing note on adaptations: Avoid literal adaptations. This is the main mistake writers make when adapting a book into a film. Film is a different medium altogether, a visual medium occurring in the present. What is important here is to serve the essence of the story, if not the literal facts. To quote a two-time Oscar-winning screenwriter:

> Here is the most important rule of adaptation: you must be totally faithful to the intention of the source material, not the source material itself.
> — William Goldman (*All the President's Men, The Princess Bride*)

Another Oscar winner, Anthony Minghella (*The English Patient*) spoke at the Getty Art Museum about adapting the novel *Cold Mountain* as a film. "The job of art is not to document but to conjure what is more true than what is true. *Cold Mountain* (the novel) is set in South Carolina but we shot it in Rumania! What has meaning is an emotional truth, not a literal truth."

I was once hired to adapt a classic novel of Finland, *Wolfbride*, into a feature screenplay. The challenge was that the novel or novella written by turn-of-the-last-century novelist Ainō Kallas — though a wonderful idea — was a bit thin as a story. It was written as a simple fairytale with very few characters. And it was written pre-Freud without any psychological allusions. "The woodcutter lived with his wife," etc. Also, note that this story about werewolves was not a horror story. Who could resist such a challenge, right? So I tried to tune into the essence of the story about a remarkable — if different — woman who falls in love with a werewolf and is burned at the stake as a witch in seventeenth-century Europe. First, I immersed myself in research of the period, both the history as well as visual images of painters of the period. The paintings of

Brueghel were especially helpful. Then I added twenty-five characters to the story and fleshed out the major characters, making
them three-dimensional. Adding psychological and erotic layers
helped as well. I was inspired by the style of Ingmar Bergman's art
films, long favorites of mine. It is said that Hollywood films are
about ordinary people in extraordinary situations while European
art films are about extraordinary people in ordinary situations.
Wolfbride combines both.

Later when I was flown over to Finland to meet the ancestor
of the long deceased novelist Aino Kallas, the director was a bit
worried, as I had taken such liberties with this known classic. A
luncheon was scheduled by the director for me to meet the ancestor who zealously guarded Kallas's reputation. It turned out that
she was very pleased and even said that the script was faithful
to the essence of the story — exactly what I had intended. All
breathed a sigh of relief as we settled down to lunch in Helsinki.

So the moral of this example is to take liberty yet serve the
story's essence.

Here's one more example of a story outline, also from a novel.
This one is a family story targeted for Disney Films or Hallmark.

Close to Heaven

by
Catherine Ann Jones
(based on the book by Faye Gibbons)

THE SETTING
Rural Georgia, 1950. Thanksgiving Week.

THE THEME
Home is where people love you.

THE CHARACTERS

DAVE LAWSON, 12

JIMMI, 11, neighbor and tomboy

GRAN & PA, Dave's rural grandparents

JOE, Dave's hound dog

BESSIE, 70s, eccentric yet wise mountain woman

JEWEL ED, Bessie's ne'er-do-well son.

RUBY, Jewel Ed's woman

WILLARD, Pa's son, Dave's uncle

HOYT, Dave's father

ELMER HULL, 70s, lives next to Hoyt's boarding house

HATTIE HULL, 60s, Elmer's bossy wife

PITTER-PAT, Elmer's pet rooster

THE STORY

Three years after his mother's death and feeling overworked and betrayed by his emotionally distant, rural grandparents, DAVE, 12, runs away to the city to find his father. JIMMI, 11, a tomboy neighbor, follows him. Together, in a perilous adventure through the Georgia mountains, a scrape with a mountain lion, and chance encounter with BESSIE, an eccentric yet wise mountain medicine woman, Dave arrives at the city for the first time in his life. He learns a valuable lesson from ELMER HULL, an elderly black man who loves a pet rooster more than anything. Finally, Dave manages to track down HOYT, his father, only to make the sad discovery that his father is a thief and the one — not his grandparents — who betrayed him by selling his mother's things.

Returning to Bessie just in time to save her life from JEWEL ED, Bessie's no good drunken son who has returned to steal his mother's hidden savings, Dave

> grows up fast. Discovering Bessie's quilt patched
> from bits of the people she has loved (Jewel Ed and
> Dave among others); Dave asks if he can stay with
> her. Bessie, truly wise, says he belongs with his
> grandparents who love and miss him, even though
> they "ain't the kind to make a big show of how they
> feel."
>
> The truth about the past helps Dave discover
> himself and realize that the grandparents he left
> behind are his "home" after all. Dave returns home
> just in time for Thanksgiving.

Notice also that there is plenty of space on the page, not overly crowded, which makes it all the easier to read. A writer's job in writing the marketing or selling story outline is to make reading it as easy as possible. It should have the same flow a good movie has. Remember that the agent or editor you are submitting your outline to has to plow through dozens of such outlines or proposals daily. Don't give him an excuse to put yours down before reading to the end.

What will make one story outline stand out above all the rest?

I assume at this point that is understood that the format is clear and professional, spelling checked, and there will now be a flow to the story after substantial rewrites.

This said, what does one look for amidst the competition: originality, a fresh voice, and passion. If you've chosen the story you can connect with emotionally, that feeling is contagious and will be felt by the reader and audience. And if it is written from your self, then it will be unique and fresh.

If your story is to have depth, the feeling must come first. When story and feeling come together, Soul is present. Writing the right story at the right time is also important. Shakespeare, again: "Ripeness is all." This is when the personal story echoes that of the collective. *Thelma and Louise* is one example; *Seabiscuit*, and *Syriana* which depicts the conflict in the Middle East through the eyes of George Clooney's character's maverick struggle against government and commercial interests. The first tapped into the feminist revolution, the second appealed to a country in economic recession, and the third to the shadow side of our government's involvement in Iraq and Iran. Listen to that inner voice — it's usually right.

> Nothing has greater power than an idea whose time has arrived.
> — Victor Hugo

As your story begins to take shape, ideas will come. Let them. The creative process is often unexpected, full of twists and turns, as your story should be.

In his book, *The Dynamics of Creation*, Anthony Storr reminds us that Sigmund Freud compared the writer's activity with that of the child at play: "A writer creates a world of fantasy which he takes very seriously—that is, which he invests with large amounts of emotion—while separating it sharply from reality."

It is important to allow the child within to play, and to feel. Play is good for Soul — and amazing art just may arise. It is not a hindrance to the discipline of writing, only a handmaiden. Both imagination — play is a form of imagination — and craft are necessary to birth a good story.

A story may arise that at first makes no realistic sense at all. Yet it may become *Edward Scissorhands, Whale Rider, The Wizard of Oz,* or *Harry Potter* — which was turned down by eight publishers before being accepted. Often an idea whose time has come may be captured first by the creatives and only much later grasped by the producers of talent. Of course, any writer wants recognition and a livelihood from his art, but it is a greater triumph to write from your soul and attract the collective.

Joseph Campbell, the famous mythologist, said, "Follow your bliss and doors will open where there were no doors before." This is literally true. Courage is needed but as artist Louise Nevelson once said, "You pay a price for what you do and you pay a price for what you don't do." Isn't it then better to follow your passion or bliss, and be true to your Soul?

EXERCISE

Develop three story outlines, one page each, using one of the sample forms already given or one of your own. Then ask yourself which one you feel most strongly about. Don't decide in a rational manner, listen to your feelings or gut instinct on this one. Later you may return to the other two, at the right time.

Here's another example of a story outline, this one for a television miniseries. In this example, I omitted the list of characters altogether, choosing to integrate character descriptions within the story itself.

THE SAI PROPHECY

By
Catherine Ann Jones
(based on the book by Barbara Gardner)

THE SETTING

Santa Barbara, Paris, Jerusalem, and Ladakh;

1899 to the present

THE THEME

The triumph of good over evil.

THE STORY

Tasmania, 1899. A dying aborigine gives anthropologist PHILO HOFFMAN an unusual ring engraved with Sanskrit words. The quest begins as PHILO later encounters a remarkable holy man in Bombay.

Thus begins a sweeping 160-year saga of romance, intrigue, tragedy, and enlightenment as five generations of the Hoffman family find their lives impacted by the three Sai Baba avatars of modern India.

Today, GINA HOFFMAN, a cynical businesswoman, inherits Philo's ring, fulfilling the destiny that connects her family with the Indian avatars. Against a background of political conspiracies, the Hoffman clan is caught up in a global game of power and corruption. This suspenseful saga moves from the breezy mansions of Santa Barbara to the steaming byways of India, from the salons of Paris to the melting pot of Jerusalem, and finally to an austere monastery in Ladakh.

As a beleaguered civilization struggles to survive during the twenty-first century, the transformation of consciousness fostered by the Sai avatars begins to take hold. But, before the Golden Age can be realized, the long awaited battle of Armageddon must be played out on a desolate, barren hilltop in the Holy Land.

Again, though these examples are all one-page outlines, they will vary in length, depending on how long the proposed project is. For a marketing tool, I would limit it to eight pages top, unless it is a mini-series which may be twice that long. Where a film will be two hours, a mini-series will be four or even six hours. Sometimes overly cautious producers will ask for more extended outlines called treatments. Here is a treatment required when I was writing *Unlikely Angel* for Disney Studios. Observe that a treatment is not literary writing, but rather a blueprint listing briefly what occurs in each scene and act breaks. It is, in fact, a kind of shorthand. You might call it a road map. It starts with Pre-Credits — that is a short scene before the screen credits appear.

UNLIKELY ANGEL

by
Catherine Ann Jones

Pre-Credits: SLEAZY COUNTRY WESTERN BAR. DOLLY sings as she notices her LOVER/BOSS slip out with a younger woman. At her break, Dolly follows and finds them necking in his truck. She quits, asking for money owed. He has very little to give. She leaves after making an oath to never work in a dump like this.

Driving too fast on a rainy night, Dolly swerves to avoid hitting a young doe, the crashes into a tree. She dies instantly.

HEAVEN. Contented angels, all save one, Dolly. Others gossip about Dolly still being homesick for earth.

Music Festival: Dolly can't get used to harp. She misses her guitar. Dolly's style of singing is too lively for the heavenly choir.

PETER (Roddy McDowell), head angel, discovers in annual audit that Dolly has not earned her wings. He considers sending her to the other place. Other angels plead for Dolly.

Peter reminds her she's failed before due to getting too involved and that this is her last chanced to leave behind her human tendencies and move on. She is reminded that the suggested rule is "no use of powers." If powers are used three times, she will automatically be sent to the other place. Dolly gulps, "Anything else?" Yes, watch out for your three temptations: food, men, and fun. You have until Christmas, only one week away.

Peter hastens Dolly's re-entry despite her now feeling not ready. "Where exactly are you sending me?" Peter tells her, "To a family in need." "What exactly am I supposed to do?" "That's your job."

Like Alice down the rabbit hole, Dolly is plopped down in an upscale Dallas neighborhood in front of a solid middle-class home. MACK opens door mistaking Dolly for someone come to interview for nanny position. Dolly takes a sharp breath when she sees Mack, a good-looking guy. "Wow!" then mutters, "This is going to be tough." Dolly goes inside pretending to be a nanny.

Dolly walks into a family in chaos, each leading separate, fragmented lives. Mack, a workaholic urban cowboy who inherited a small family gift store, is opening his third branch store. Since his divorce three years ago, Mack has not let anyone get close, even shutting out his own children.

The two children are bickering as they pack to join their mother in France for Christmas.

Dolly meets SAM, 7 going on 35, whose only friends are indoors on the Internet. Sam has no social skills or even interest in real, embodied people.

Dolly meets JUDY, 15, a slender, insecure beauty, who talks on the phone all the time about the big question, "When and to whom will we lose it to?" Judy, too, has become the woman of the house in place of an absent mother.

Judy shares a secret plan to ask her Mom if she can move to France. Texas is old news. Patsy is envious.

Mack reminds children that they leave early morning for airport. Patsy reluctantly leaves.

Mack interviews Dolly, informing her she would start work January 1st. Sam and Judy comment she sure doesn't look like any nanny they've ever seen.

Ex-wife SUSAN phones to cancel her children's trip to France. Her new lover, BERTRAND, insists on taking her to south of France alone.

Mack is furious as he's super busy with work. Judy is especially disappointed but masks it, later blowing up at Dolly who understands how disappointed she must be.

Dolly, eager to succeed in her mission this time, quickly offers to move in early, and spend

Christmas with the family.

ELAINE, Mack's sales manager for stores, drops by
to tell him he's needed to make decisions about new
branch store. Dolly and Elaine meet briefly.

Mack asks Elaine's advice. Elaine suggests he let
her stay a week for a trial run. Mack thinks it a
good idea and tells Dolly who agrees. Mack leaves
for the store, leaving her two charges glaring at
her.

End of Act I

ACT II

Judy shows Dolly the house. Trying to be
sophisticated like her Mom, she thinks Dolly is
corny. Too "up" all the time. Judy says she'll
be living in Paris soon with her mother though
admits her mother doesn't know this as yet. Dolly
notices a family photograph. Judy explains that was
their home when Mother was still with us. "It's at
the lake not far from here." Dolly remarks, "It's
beautiful" and Judy lets her veil drop for a moment
as she responds. Dolly learns that Mack's parents
are dead but wonders why no photos are displayed.
Judy says they weren't particularly close.

Dolly, happy to be back on earth, thinks this
is the real heaven. She delights in every little
thing. Taking Sam with her to buy groceries, he
thinks she's nuts to enjoy shopping. Dolly loves
dark chocolate. Dolly tries unsuccessfully to reach
Sam who is lost in his portable computer baseball
game. When Dolly asks if he ever plays baseball
outside, he looks at her as if she's crazy.

Family dinner. Dolly notices there is no Christmas
tree yet. They say they never celebrate Christmas.
They're usually traveling somewhere. Dolly remarks
her fondest memories are of Christmas with her
family, but dodges when they ask about her past.

Sam leaves, taking plate with him to eat with his
computer game. Judy gets phone call from Patsy

which leaves Mack and Dolly at table. Mack says he inherited store from his Dad. Dolly, awkward being alone with Mack, drops her knife. They both reach down to pick it up, bump their heads then look at one another under the table. Dolly, already smitten, breathes too quickly. Mack shyly makes a quick movement banging his head.

Dolly insists the children help her choose a Christmas tree. Mack makes them go. Approached by a probable mugger, children are amazed when Dolly sweet talks the mugger.

Dolly glimpses a poster announcing a hoedown square dance.

The children are exhausted by Dolly's tireless energy. She seems to be enjoying everything, having been away. The children begin to wonder, "Where has she been?"

A moment later, some dogs stop fighting in her presence. One of the dogs follows them home. Dolly tells children they should adopt him. She calls him Rupert to help her stay on track. Children are totally indifferent to new dog.

Dolly makes a list of all the things on earth she's missed and wants to do. Why, there won't be time enough!

Later, Dolly causes further distance between her and children by telling them what she thinks, what they should do like having family dinner together. They tell her she can't tell them what to do. They decide Dolly's passé and positively weird, a threat to the status quo. Maybe she's been locked up in prison, maybe she's a psycho nanny like in the movies! The children determine to find out who she really is. Sam says he can break into the police records on his computer. Judy will snoop in her room, Dog Rupert follows Sam.

End of Act II

ACT III

Dolly concocts a clever ruse to get the family to hoedown.

HOEDOWN. Bar-B-Q at covered wagon, barn square dance. Dolly, who never had enough dancing before she died, is the life of the party. Sam, void of social skills, stands apart observing. Judy tries to appear bored until a handsome rancher's son, MIKE, 16, asks her to dance. Mack is amazed at Dolly's endless energy when she's having fun. He is also captivated by her special smell, essence of roses, yet resists falling in love as they slow dance with the moon.

MOONLIT HAYRIDE. Sam has a pocket computer game. Judy is with Mike.

Mack feels like a teenager again, relaxes, and has fun. Never got to do much as a teenager as he had to work after school at his Dad's store. Dog Rupert makes contact with Sam who still avoids people. Dolly suggests Mack do things with Sam. He loves that computer baseball but never plays it live. Didn't your Dad play catch with you? Mack says, "Once" — but doesn't explain further.

Back home after hot chocolate, Judy phones Patsy, mentions meeting Mike. Though of course he's not her type, she can't help talking about him.

Sam cuts a few square dance steps alone with dog Rupert before turning on computer. Dolly observes but doesn't let on how delighted she is. Dog sleeps in Sam's room. Dolly feels great, not wanting to ever leave the earth.

Dolly discovers Mack's secret music room in basement. Mack's secret passion is to be a singer with guitar. Dolly is happy to find a guitar — though not a very good one.

Mack at first angry at his secret room being invaded but is enticed by Dolly to join her singing and playing. This draws them closer together. Dolly gets overheated by her strong attraction to Mack which he feels, too. Candles glow especially strong as their eyes meet and ignite causing another glow amidst the candles.

Mack tries to find out who she is. "You're not like anyone I've ever known." Dolly confesses she was a singer once, but that was a long time back. When Mack asks where and when, Dolly dodges. Mack, a master of control, doesn't like not knowing. He is convinced she is hiding something.

Next morning. Dolly tries to get children to help her decorate the tree but they think the whole idea is corny. Judy is furious when Dolly interferes with her scheme to seduce Mike and lose her virginity. Dolly says making love is not a fad. Both Sam and Judy insist that what they need is to be left alone! Sam gives insight that we've always been left to ourselves. It's what we're used to. Dolly responds, "That's the saddest thing I've ever heard." Judy and Sam speed up their search to uncover Dolly's real identity.

Sam's TEACHER phones to say Sam has missed two rehearsals. Sam is cast as Joseph in the school Christmas pageant as he's the tallest. He doesn't want to as he doesn't like to leave his room, and the Mary scares him. Why? She keeps smiling at me all the time.

Dolly thinks it's a great idea and bribes Sam with a new computer game to help him see the pageant through. Dolly admits that all this computer stuff is new to her. Sam is sure she's been in prison.

After dropping a reluctant Sam off, Dolly takes Judy shopping at a giant mall surrounding an ice rink. Christmas is everywhere. Judy buys clothes for herself as if she were her mother. Dolly wonders why Mack has no girlfriends. Why did he shut down, closed his heart, was it the divorce? Judy says even before he was kind of distant.

They collect Sam at school auditorium. Dog Rupert runs towards Sam just as a large truck turns the corner. Dolly, against Peter's orders, uses her powers to stop the truck in order to save the dog. The children see Dolly hit yet remain unharmed. They panic and run, believing her now to be a witch. "I'm out of here!" "Me, too!"

Dolly tries to follow the children but loses them.

At home, Dolly faces the undecorated tree then flips out as she considers how to tell Mack his children are gone. Dolly is becoming emotionally involved (her old failing!) and is surprised how much she cares what Mack thinks of her. At this moment, a porcelain angel ornament falls and breaks at Dolly's feet. Dolly picks up the pieces then looks up, knowing it's a sign from Peter. She calls his name but he does not appear.

CLOSE on calendar announcing, Three Days Before Christmas. Dolly, knowing she has once again made a mess of it, loses hope.

End of Act III

(SKIP Act IV-Act VI)

Rupert comes to collect Dolly who refuses to leave until a suitable replacement is found. "I can't abandon this family. They love me and I love them. This family needs a good woman and I'm not leaving until we find one — even if I forfeit my wings forever!"

End of Act VI

ACT VII

Elaine drops by with her Christmas gift: an angel to place on top of their tree. It's one of her collection. Dolly sees that Elaine is the one. To insure their happiness, Dolly secretly showers Elaine with her special smell, essence of roses. Dolly tells Elaine she wants her to do something for Mack and the family.

Dolly leaves gifts under the tree. As they sleep, a transformed Dolly kisses the children goodbye.

One last look at Mack, also asleep.

Dolly is at peace at long last, knowing even though she's failed herself (earning her wings), that the family will be all right. Smiling, a contented Dolly falls asleep.

Dolly experiences visions of angels, heavenly choirs. She awakens infused with Light. Accepting at last that her time as a human being has come to a close, it's time to move on. Dolly understands that it is her unselfish love that has won the day.

CHRISTMAS MORNING. Rupert the dog wakes first and finds his big bone tied with a red ribbon.

Sam wakes Judy to tell her Dolly is gone. At first upset, they find her gifts under the tree. Outside Elaine, following Dolly's instructions, brings Grandpa who is delighted to find a box of Butterfingers under the tree.

Mike shows up with a gift. Judy asks Mike to stay.

Mack discovers a new guitar. He and the children suddenly notice that the angel atop the tree is glowing. When Sam wonders if Dolly got anything for Christmas, the little angel glows and expands into Dolly in the sky, complete with wings.

HEAVEN. Dolly, with wings and a glowing presence, asks Peter if Mack will be happy and is surprised when he says, "That's up to you, my dear." Peter then assigns her to be Mack's guardian angel for life and the children. Dolly, her hair blowing in the wind, white fluffy clouds roll by, as she watches over "her family." She sings, "Whenever Forever Comes."

Sam tries on his new baseball glove and is surprised when his Dad offers to play catch. "You know how to play?" Mack replies, "I used to. My Dad taught me." Father and son play catch in the yard as Grandpa looks up, eating a Butterfinger.

Mike and Judy sit on the porch in the swing, and talk, holding hands.

Dolly smiles as Mack smelling the essence of roses does a double take and sees Elaine as if for the first time. Elaine smiles.

Peter tells Dolly that he has larger missions ahead for her. After all, her work is only beginning.

The End

Once you have a draft of your story outline, stay with it for as long as you can stand it. It is a good idea to re-write it several times, thus creating a solid story structure. With each successive draft, edit out what is not needed. Tighten. Focus on revealing the main character, ambiance or setting, and, of course, the theme.

Novels vary in length as well, but please note that this suggested outline will help to structure any form of narrative writing. They are the bare bones; later you add the real meat.

> After writing movies for thirty-five years, I am more convinced than ever it's only about story.
> — William Goldman

Remember, that though there is no guarantee that you will ever write a great story, one thing is certain: you will never write a great story until you write a story. Writing, like life, is a process, and the process has just begun.

> Today is the first day of the rest of your life.
> — Abbie Hoffman

Chapter 4

Tracking Story Specifics:
The Secret to Successful Rewrites

I didn't have time to write it shorter.
— Woodrow Wilson

EACH WRITER DISCOVERS his own writing process because, in the final count, writing is not something to learn but something to do. There is no one right method to the writing process. Each and every writer must discover his own rhythm. Some write endings first, while others write detailed outlines, structuring the whole before beginning page one. Tom Stoppard, the English playwright and co-writer of the Oscar-winning film *Shakespeare in Love*, says he begins a play by hearing the voices of the characters talking, and has no idea of any plot.

It is fine for one writer to begin writing a first scene and have no idea where it will end up while another may start with the ending and work backwards. Another may rewrite sentences or scenes as he goes, perfecting before moving on. Furthermore, each and every play or book by the same author may be written in an entirely different manner. The way and form must serve the material — and not the other way round. As long as the story is completed, it matters little how it got there. Experience — that is, the regular practice of writing — will help you to discover your way. That said, let me try to be helpful by sharing my approach, acknowledging that it is just one of the many paths to Rome — or Hollywood.

After writing and re-writing the story outline, I prefer to jump in and write a rough first draft, rather like a snow ball rolling down hill, stopping at nothing. Only after completing a rough draft will I invite my inner critic to sit on my shoulder and become a welcomed ally in the re-writing process. This is also when outside readers are invited to look and comment.

Before a first draft is completed, I suggest you lock your inner critic (usually the internalized voice of a parent) in a closet and leave him there until later. Though constructive at the appropriate time, an inner critic can become an obstacle to the writing.

> I've missed more than 9,000 shots in my career. I've lost almost 300 games. Twenty-six times, I've been trusted to take the game-winning shot and missed. I've failed over and over and over again in my life. And that is why I succeed.
> — Michael Jordan

Here, I speak from my own experience as well. Any writer — regardless of how many awards and successes — has endured failures or almost successes. Hopefully, however, he will learn from the failures. John Bishop wrote a fine play, *The Trip Back Down,* which closed its first week on Broadway. It is the story of a famous race car driver who, older now, is beginning to lose races. He returns to his small hometown and someone criticizes him for losing a recent big race. He turns to the man who has never left home, and says, "Just remember, in order to lose, you have to be in the race."

Sadly, the inner critic may surface quite early in a career. When I was an undergraduate, I delayed writing my first play, thinking, "It can't compare with Chekhov or Shakespeare, so why bother?" Not the most constructive attitude for a beginning writer. Then a lucky thing happened. I learned that the University of Texas at Austin had a fine collection of original manuscripts by such renowned authors as Samuel Beckett, Dylan Thomas, George Bernard Shaw, and Tennessee Williams, among many others. I also learned that you could obtain a pass to sit and read them in an authorized room. Epiphany! I observed that Dylan Thomas would cross out one word twenty times until finding the one right word. In other words, a great published poem like *Fern Hill* by Dylan Thomas, does not arise perfect from the writer's mind, like Botticelli's Venus from the sea, but has undergone several drafts first. At eighteen, this fact was a godsend. Holding in my hands the original manuscript of Shaw's *Pygmalion*, seeing the playwright's hand slicing and adding words, spurred me on when I most needed it. For a writer, libraries are sacred temples in which to realize a hidden destiny. It goes without saying that in order to write well, you must read well. That includes all those interested in writing screenplays, for, as I would tell my graduate film students at the University of Southern California, it is not sufficient simply to view movies. Why? Because screenplays — as other forms of narrative — are written with words.

Once in a *Paris Review* interview, Ernest Hemingway was asked how much rewriting he did. He replied, "It depends. I rewrote the ending of *Farewell to Arms*, the last page of it, thirty-nine times before I was satisfied."

Interviewer: "Was there some technical problem? What was it that had stumped you?" Hemingway replied, "Getting the words right."

Hence, any writer worth his salt will spend adequate time reading and fine-tuning his craft, becoming a wordsmith. And, remember, what you cut, can't fail. The deliciously funny P. G. Wodehouse, who gave us *Jeeves,* once said, "I suppose the secret of writing is to go through your stuff till you come on something you think is particularly good, and then cut it out."

Kill your darlings.
— Ernest Hemingway

The best advice I can give for successful re-writing is to target specifics. If story is about everything then it's about nothing. *The universal lies in the specific and not the other way round.* Don't write about a dog but a sheltie. Use research for fiction as well as nonfiction narratives. Use libraries and the Web; call or write directly to experts in the field you are writing about. Police officers, physicians, scientists, Vietnam vets, etc., are usually generous with their time. Just call and say you are writing a novel or film about Alzheimer's disease, for instance, as I did for the Sundance film, *Angel Passing*, starring Hume Cronyn and Calista Flockhart. Ask them if you might call them at a convenient time and talk with them for a few minutes. I have never had a refusal. It might be a person who has lived what your main character will, such as a drug addict or a soldier who fought in Iraq or Vietnam. People are surprisingly generous with their time, and they also usually don't mind talking about themselves!

Dare to be personal. What is the emotional personal thread from your own life which can be woven into your story? Answer this, and you will have the key to meaning for yourself as the writer as well as for the audience, who will identify with your feeling. It is no coincidence that the greatest novels and plays are often inspired by the author's own family background. Eugene O'Neill's *Long Day's Journey into Night*, Tennessee Williams' *The Glass Menagerie*, Boris Pasternak's *Dr. Zhivago,* or Thomas Wolfe's *Look Homeward Angel* are all examples of this form of inspiration. Fiction is often referred to as disguised autobiography. A more recent film, *The Pursuit of Happyness*, based on the true story of Chris Gardner, played by Will Smith, is another.

The family drama is a more tightened space, observing one of the classic unities: setting. The other two unities, according to Aristotle, are one central action and the entire story occurring within a twenty-four-hour period.

Subjectivity is necessary for all great art. Story is no exception. I will go on record and say that subjective point of view from the writer as well as the subjective response of reader or audience is the most important aspect of any book or movie. This is why sometimes our favorite movies or books are not classics, but simply something we strongly identify with. They hit a nerve. A disaster film depicting a great love story, *Titanic* became the top-grossing movie of all time. One of my favorites is *Anne of Green Gables* about a little girl with too much imagination. Ask yourself what is your favorite book or movie, the one you like to return to, and it may surprise you that it may not be a great classic, but simply the book or movie you love.

Craft without art: it works but who cares? The audience must care. Caring sells tickets. We care by identifying with the main character, something within must emotionally connect to our own life. Again, dare to be personal.

When television producer, Martha Williamson, invited me to write for her hit series, *Touched by an Angel*, I said I preferred to make up my original stories. She asked me to make up a few and pitch them to her. She told me that if she did not like any of my stories, she would give me a story to write. I pitched nine original stories, and the one she chose for me to write first was the only one of the nine that was inspired by an incident from my own life. I was psychic as a child and would often tune out and listen to inner music, so my teacher thought I might be hard of hearing. This diagnosis began a series of doctors and examinations to find out what was wrong with me. Of course, nothing was wrong. I was simply creatively entering into my own world. So this was the starting point for what became the episode, *A Joyful Noise*. It is about a little girl who hears angels singing and is sent to a psychiatrist to rid her of her voices. In the end, it is the psychiatrist who is changed by the little girl and her angels. Olympia Dukakis plays an archangel in this episode. This was one of Oprah's favorites — she once screened a clip on her weekly television show. So, the moral is: Dare to be personal.

These works, cut from our own past, are sometimes the toughest to write because to write our own stories brings up ghosts and long buried emotions. In writing my early plays, I avoided the one play I knew I had one day to write: the inevitable dysfunctional family play. *The Women of Cedar Creek* came about like this.

After seeing four of my plays produced, the family play began to make itself known, a gentle tapping at my chamber door. Still I resisted by not sitting down to write the play. However, I did begin to save scraps of dialogue and character details. Out of nowhere, bits of dialogue would pop up in the recesses of the mind and I would dutifully jot them down, tossing them into a shoebox in my

New York apartment. After a few months, I had quite a pile. Then I was invited to Yaddo, an art colony in Sarasota Springs, New York, to write. It was clear that I could not put this play off any longer though the inner child was still somewhat reluctant to tackle these early Texas years. Arriving at Yaddo, I asked for a large bulletin board and tacks. Then at the top of the board I tacked on slips of paper, each bearing the name of one of six characters. Then under each character's name, I pinned the collected scraps of dialogue. Pretty soon, I had a board covered with dialogue and six characters in search of an author. This would soon become *The Women of Cedar Creek* — three generations of Texas women. I knew that this was a story which had to come out, for therapeutic reasons, if not art. I had no illusions about selling this one. I simply had to get it out of my system. So during my Yaddo stay, I wrote a very specific play about growing up in Texas and being formed by powerful Southern women who were at war with themselves and each other. At the end, it was as if a ghost had been exorcised. I was free of the past and could move on. Imagine my surprise when that play went on to win the New York Drama League Award, Julie Harris Award, and the Beverly Hills Theatre Guild Award! People would see the play and say, "I'm from Kansas, and that's my family exactly. However did you know?"

In this way, I learned that the universal is carried by a specific place and specific characters. Anton Chekov was a master of the specific. He wrote about provincial Russia and his themes and characters are as universally true today as when written over a century ago.

Never forget that the best tools you have as a writer are yourself, your memories, your values, your POV or life perspective, your doubts, fears, and obsessions. Especially your doubts, fears, and obsessions! This alone makes your story unique. Write from yourself, not from what you think the market dictates. These stories take tremendous courage as they arise from your very soul. These stories will carry the power of the gods and result in universal, archetypal myths. Please understand that I am not advocating literally writing your own life story — though you may wish to do this. I am encouraging you to tap into your feelings about your own memories and imbue those passions and fears and sorrows into your fictional or non-fictional story. My Texas play is not a literal representation of my family of origin, but I used place and prototypes to make the play real, first to me and then later to an audience. You must invest your own feelings, fears, and conflicts in order to birth an authentic story.

> Whatever our theme in writing, it is old and tried ... It is only
> the vision that can be new, but that is enough.
> — Eudora Welty

It might be helpful to talk of starting points. They may differ from work to work, and usually do. The writer's mind functions as a kind of radar, ever ready to detect a possible seed. For instance, what got me started on the play, *The Women of Cedar Creek*, was a phone call from my mother describing a group of widows spending the weekend together at a Texas resort. Shortly thereafter, I abandoned the idea of the widows and made it a three-generation family play based loosely on the women in my own family: a grandmother, mother, two aunts, a daughter, and their maid. These starting points serve to begin the process. It matters little if the horse changes its color on the journey. The idea that fascinated me was that a family can say and do terrible things to each other and usually do, yet, at the end of the day, sit down and eat roast beef together as though nothing were out of the ordinary.

Remember Aristotle? I borrowed his classic unities of time, space, and theme, and was on my way. That is, the play took place in one setting, one twenty-four-hour period, and was about one thing: the destructive and unifying bond of family.

In the beginning, you may — like Tennessee Williams — start with a character and only after writing a draft, discover your theme. Or the theme may start you off, as with Arthur Miller's plays. Sooner or later, what you are writing about, especially if you feel strongly about it, will make itself known to you. Find the unifying thread to weave the pieces of your story. Therein is the key to a successful story. It is best to choose a theme that you feel strongly about. In this way, your story is re-visioned and transformed into universal literature.

Now, to approach the task of re-writing, crucial to any good story. The first step in this process, for me, is to set aside the story, play, or screenplay, for at least two weeks. Try to not even think about it. This provides a necessary distance for later, when it is time to unlock that inner critic — allowing him input at last.

Re-writing separates the aspiring writer from the professional one. (It may be useful to copy and create a new computer file as Story2, before rewriting. Later if you change your mind, you have preserved the original text.) The first step in re-writing is tracking. Tracking is a method which can help focus your story during several read-throughs and consequent re-writes. There are different ways to approach tracking. Tracking theme is but one, but let us start with theme.

> Writing and rewriting are a constant search for what you are trying to say.
> — John Updike

What is theme? Theme is the meaning, both rational and emotional, of our viewing or reading experience. It is based on the emotional drive of your main character and his resolution of — or failure to resolve — this drive. Be careful. A word of caution here. One of the early movie moguls, Sam Goldwyn, said, "If you've got a message, send it by Western Union." Themes are best served through the emotional response of your audience, not by preaching or being too much on the nose, as Uta Hagen, my former acting teacher, would say.

In the Oscar-winning script *Good Will Hunting*, the Matt Damon character finds himself through his relationship with the psychiatrist played by Robin Williams (who also won an Oscar for this performance). The theme: Finding your place in the world without becoming a slave to success. The character never overtly states this message but you feel it by the end of the film. And you are moved when he drives away from a substantial job opportunity for the woman he loves. This story is all about feeling, something we have been carefully educated away from, yet go to the movies to reclaim.

Again, sometimes we may not know the theme — what the story is really about — until a first draft has been written. Once the theme is clear you can go back and track it throughout the story, book, or screenplay. Use theme as a roadmap, focusing on it exclusively as you do a read-through of your draft. Ask these questions, as you do the read-through: Does each scene serve the overall theme? Or, in other words, what is your story really about?

The award-winning play and film *Amadeus* provides an excellent example. *Amadeus* is a play, not about Mozart, but about envy. Mozart and eighteenth-century Europe are merely the venue or backdrop to the drama of Salieri's obsessive envy of his rival, Mozart. And envy is as relevant today as in Mozart's time. Here is the key to successful period stories: Choose universal themes. Theme or moral revelation is what's missing in most Hollywood films as well as contemporary novels. Read through the draft and think only about envy. Does each scene as well as your dialogue underscore that specific theme? If not, or if it does not reveal character or push the plot forward, you may be facing words that should be cut.

> A play should make a single striking point ... one smashing explosion.
> — Tennessee Williams

Another American playwright, Arthur Miller, felt strongly about the injustice of the McCarthy witch hunts where idealistic writers were hunted down and disgraced, often losing their livelihoods. So he wrote a play about a seventeenth-century witch hunt, *The Crucible*. The passion Miller poured into this period story was full of present parallels, as most good period stories are. Be faithful to the essence, if not the actual facts.

As an aspiring actress, I was once directed by Arthur Miller in the Broadway tryout in Philadelphia of another of his plays, *Death of a Salesman* with George C. Scott and Teresa Wright. Over apple pie and tea, Miller discussed his life with me. As others I have known irrevocably imprinted by the McCarthy era, Miller spoke about the injustice as if it had happened the week before. This deep feeling is pure gold for a writer. Feed it, use it. Never forget that people go to theatre and films to feel something. And first, the writer must feel before a reader or audience will.

Another way to track and rewrite is to cut out anything that does not serve the emotional payoff. What is it that you wish the reader or audience to feel? Anger? Pathos? Joy? Sexual excitement? Sorrow?

Incidentally, Miller mentioned to me that the prototype of the salesman, Willie Loman, was an uncle of his who actually was a salesman. One way a story rings true is to incorporate settings we know well, as well as character prototypes and how they speak.

In 2003, HBO aired a six-and-a-half-hour adaptation of the Pulitzer Prize–winning play, *Angels in America*. What has sustained the devotion to this play for the past eighteen years? At first look, the story is about AIDS in America, but on a closer look, it is about much more. The real themes of the play are about love and betrayal, commitment and fear of the unknown. And it is about sexual politics, as well. Playwright Tony Kushner adds that his play is "about the liberation of the democratic citizen." Is there anyone that this play does not cover? Here a specific story expands to universal themes. In the specific lies the universal, and not the other way round. So once you know what you are trying to say, your theme becomes your focus, and the best guide to re-writing.

To give another example, let us look again at the best-seller book and film, *Seabiscuit*. The movie, incidentally, is not about the horse. It masterfully tracks three men's lives brought together by the horse, Seabiscuit. The background of the story is America during the depression of the 1930s. The theme is the same as the popular children's book, *The Little Engine That Could*. The theme of both is never giving up on your dream. Historically, Americans in the 1930s, some of whom had lost everything, latched onto the story of *Seabiscuit* as a metaphor of not giving up, even when you're licked. As Americans endure economic uncertainty, this parallel works as well today.

The three men — owner, trainer, and jockey — have all had hard knocks of one kind or another but they keep on, join together, and win the brass ring — or winner's cup. Now you don't need to have ridden a horse or been to a racetrack to emotionally connect with this book or film. Who hasn't known failure and the feeling of hopelessness, and who doesn't want to feel that if he can do it, then so can I! That sentiment is what sells this book and film.

The chances are that something you feel strongly about may find a mirrored response in the collective. After all, the personal and the collective are interconnected, as even the scientists tell us today.

When I speak of using your feelings and drawing from real-life settings, characters, and dialogue, please do not be encouraged to write it down just like it happened. Unless you are writing an autobiography — and even then, some heightening is usually prescribed — it is crucial to remember that a great story is not a realistic photograph but rather an Impressionist oil painting. What really happened must be transposed into literature. The agent for this alchemical work is the imagination. Imagination blended with real-life memories or knowledge can make a great story. Just putting down everything like it was is more an accountant's way of writing.

> Movies are life with the boring parts cut out.
> — Alfred Hitchcock

A good re-write requires a certain ruthlessness. Here is where your inner critic is invaluable. Sometimes it might be your favorite line which must be cut. Why? Because it simply doesn't work. In time, instinct will serve. It is a good practice to exercise this instinctive muscle when reading or viewing writings written by other writers. You'll know when something doesn't work because it usually sticks out like a sore thumb. The trick is to then ask yourself why it doesn't work. It might be overwritten or the characters simply might not ring true. Or they would never speak such dialogue. The more you become accustomed to what doesn't work, the more you can avoid the traps yourself.

I never did it, but always wanted to screen a simply awful film for my graduate film students as USC. Why? When you see a great movie, you're usually swept away and may forget to exercise a critical eye. However, when you are subjected to a bad movie, you are critical and in a far better position to see why something does not work. Here's a humorous example.

My son, Christopher, was a freshman in college, and was telling me that his friends would rag on him because he had never seen a porn movie. I immediately responded by saying, "Neither have I. Why don't we see one?" My maternal logic was saying that if I did not make a big deal about it, it would lose its appeal. Well, my son said, "Sure." So off we go to see *Emmanuelle* at a local theater near campus. Twenty minutes into this popular soft porn movie, my son leans over and says, "Mother, this is awful. Can we leave?" Outside the theatre, my son — brought up on great movies and Broadway plays — says, "That was awful. The script was bad, the acting stank, and the direction was even worse." I smiled and suggested we go see a current French art film playing nearby, which we did.

Rewriting is about serving the whole. Sometimes a scene or line may be interesting in itself, yet doesn't serve the whole. What interrupts the flow of the story? Cut. What becomes preachy? Cut. What sounds pretentious? Cut. And so on.

> Art is the elimination of the unnecessary.
> — Pablo Picasso

Another form of tracking, apart from tracking theme as previously discussed, is to focus on the single desire of your main character. Simply following the main desire can help you find the structure of your story. Remember to pay attention not only to what the character does, but why he does it. This way motive increases — why he does what he does — and generates dramatic action. Scarlett O'Hara's obsessive love for Ashley Wilkes is one example. She wants him to move to Atlanta to work in her new lumber business because she needs him to be near her. In other words, knowing the desire of your main character provides motive for his actions.

Perhaps it is a good idea to say something about dramatic action. Quite often when teaching graduate screenwriting at USC Film School in Los Angeles, I would have to make the distinction between dramatic action and physical action. When you are watching a movie and the character jumps in a car and drives recklessly away chased by three police cars, this is physical action — not necessarily dramatic action. Dramatic action is what happens between the central characters on an emotional level. In fact, the car chase probably interrupts the dramatic action. Though you may be entertained by a car chase, you are seldom deeply moved.

Several years ago, I was invited to accompany my dancer friend, Violette Verdy, to Saratoga Springs, New York, where, along with Edward Villella — also a principal dancer for George Ballanchine's New York City Ballet — she would be receiving an honorary doctorate from Skidmore University. When Eddie accepted his doctorate, he said, "Dancing is one part inspiration and ninety-nine part perspiration."

> Constant work is the law of art.
> — Balzac

This is certainly true of all the arts, including writing. Arthur Miller told me once that he did over thirty drafts of his fine play, *Death of a Salesman*. That's a lot of work. That's a lot of play!

> Too many pieces of music finish too long after the end.
> — Igor Stravinsky

What happens when you're sick of reading your story after considerable re-writes? I often put aside a work after completing a first or second draft and let it simmer for two or three weeks. What is interesting here is that something keeps working in my brain on a subliminal level. Then when I go back to the pages, I'm fresher and in a better position to objectively continue the process of rewriting. Writing is re-writing.

In Hollywood, to promote a film, studios will come up with a "log line" which is one sentence to hook the audience when they see it on a poster. This one sentence — or "high concept" — should reveal what kind of story it is and pull the audience or reader in. Not all stories can be reduced to one or two sentences but those that can usually sell more easily. Here's one example. The film *Panic in Needle Park*: Romeo and Juliet on drugs. Here are some Oscar-winning examples:

Schindler's List — A Catholic war profiteer flourishes by sucking up to the Nazis and later goes broke by employing and saving the lives of more than a thousand Polish Jews.

Forrest Gump — A dumpling wins the day. Life is a box of chocolates: you never know what you're going to get.

The Verdict — David and Goliath. Justice wins, restoring faith to an alcoholic lawyer.

To Kill a Mockingbird (Horton Foote's Oscar-winning screenplay adaptation of Harper Lee's novel) — Southern lawyer defends a black man falsely accused of rape as his children learn of life and morality.

Dances with Wolves (winner of several Oscars) — An idealistic Civil War veteran makes friends with Sioux tribe, eventually becoming one of them.

Thelma and Louise — Female friends leave responsibilities behind and hit the road, becoming fugitives from the law.

Tootsie — An obnoxious New York actor finally finds work disguised as a woman, and finds himself a better man for having been a woman.

My Best Friend's Wedding — Julia Roberts discovers her best friend/ex-boyfriend is getting married, and has only four days to win him back.

The Queen — Queen Elizabeth (Helen Mirren) loses popular support by her lack of feeling when Princess Diana, no longer a member of the royal family, is suddenly killed in a car crash. The dignity of a monarch is tested by her people and their spokesman, Tony Blair.

This is called "high concept" in Hollywood, easy to pitch, easy to sell.

Once I pitched a story idea for a feature comedy-drama to Universal Studios. I had not yet written anything down but presented the story in just two sentences. Here they are: *Sammy and Son* is a comedy about a mother and son who are roommates in college. It's a story about a son who learns how to be young and a mother who finally grows up.

Both Disney and Universal entered a bidding war which Universal won, and paid me a lot of money to write the movie. Stories like this are easier to sell as they can be reduced to one or two sentences. Incidentally, the story is inspired by a true incident. I was invited to teach at the university where my son was attending. He suggested we be housemates, and we were for one semester. (I don't recommend this as a model for parents and teenagers!) So the premise is taken from life, then exaggerated into a fictional story and characters.

The following exercises are deceptively simple, but carry the kernel of what your story is about. In my workshops, these exercises often prove the toughest even though they are the shortest. Remember theme is more than a statement. It must have emotional power. You might want to have your first sentence say what your story is about, and your second, what the theme is.

EXERCISE

Write in one or two sentences what your story is about. Include your theme.

This is a story about ...

EXERCISE

After reading a story or viewing a video or film, ask yourself what the theme of this story is, in one or two sentences. Good training for when you are writing your own.

EXERCISE

The moral dilemma of this story is ....

Track your story by focusing on plot line, following the central desire of the main character. In *Chariots of Fire*, it is winning the gold medal at the Olympics, but the story is about how that alters the main characters and their relationships. The thru-line is what carries you and the audience all the way through the story. Think of the thru-lines as the trunk supporting all the branches and leaves, or all the characters and scenes. Such thru-lines provide the central structure or spine to your story — its focus.

Don't forget that the best plots and themes emerge from character, and not the other way round. So let us take a deeper look at this crucial part of any story: character. Read through your draft focusing only on the relationship of your main characters. Track the emotional thru-line between them, thinking of nothing else. This will enable you to intensify the fuel of your story. Remember, too, that what matters in a story is not what happens as much as how what happens affects and changes your main character for better or for worse, and how it alters his behavior to others.

Track your story by the best gauge of all: What is authentic? What is not? Where did I betray my feelings? Let this Geiger counter of integrity alert you as to what to change or cut.

I often compare the writing process to a figurative painter. First he will do a pencil sketch which he changes and changes before going to oil. The Broadway stage director, George Abbot, once said to the actors, "Get up on stage and do something so we can change it."

Summon the courage to make mistakes, essential in any creative process. Go out on a limb in early drafts. If not now, when? Write to express, not to impress. Allow your main character to have his way with you in the early drafts. Let him surprise you.

I must tell you that sometimes writing the early drafts is the best time of all. Alone in your corner, lost in the world you have created, before others — who claim to know better — tell you how to write your story.

Think wrongly if you please, but in all cases think for yourself.
    — Doris Lessing

Chapter 5

Creating Character–Driven Stories

In the faces of men and women, I see God.
— Walt Whitman

THE ORIGIN OF the word "character" had to do with the craft of engraving a sign in stone. This sign (character) would in turn reference a specific, visual image. Similarly, it is the manifestation or imprint of character that reveals story. In fact, character is the heart and center of any story. In the best of cases, your main character should be a clear projected image of your story and theme. Sophie in William Styron's novel, *Sophie's Choice*, is an excellent example of a character that personifies the heart of the story. Sophie — beautifully played by Meryl Streep in the feature film version — is a stunning composite of the horrors of Nazi concentration camps. There is no need to preach the message. It is vividly present. A reader or audience has only to experience Styron's unforgettable Sophie. Through the force of character, the message is imprinted forever on both reader and audience. Who could forget the flashback scene at the camp when Sophie is asked by a Nazi soldier to choose which of her two children will live? This one moment changes the character's life forever.

The strongest principle of growth lies in human choice.
— George Eliot

Always let character carry your theme. If the reader or audience feels for the character, then your message has been delivered in a lasting manner. Character is central to all forms of narrative, both fiction and nonfiction.

One can't love humanity. One can only love people.
— Graham Greene

In Hollywood where I ply my trade, film deals are made by pitching your stories. The best stories are carried by one or two central characters. So it is often best to pitch character. Today novels and biographies are often chosen by publishers with an eye to a possible movie sale. This means a role that is a suitable star vehicle. Meryl Streep did not hesitate to say yes to the title role in *Sophie's Choice*, which incidentally won her an Oscar. Pitching a great character role in Hollywood helps to attract a star actor — essential for getting a green light in Hollywood. Another example might be As *Good As It Gets*. Try to imagine this story without Jack Nicholson, who plays the main character. There would be no story. Here the character is the story. Yes, Nicholson also won an Oscar for this role. The same is true with David Peoples' script, *Unforgiven,* written decades before megastar Clint Eastwood discovered it and committed to it. Why did he commit? It was the role of a lifetime. Jamie Fox won the Oscar for best actor for his portrayal of Ray Charles in *Ray.*

What makes a good story? The answer covers all genres whether romantic comedy, drama, or tragedy. It is no accident that the great novels or best films are character-driven stories: *Dr. Zhivago, Lawrence of Arabia, Forrest Gump, Driving Miss Daisy, Braveheart, Annie Hall, Erin Brockovich, and The Queen.* Note again that these examples carry the main character in the titles.

As previously mentioned, *Gone with the Wind* is not about the Civil War — that is merely the backdrop or venue for the real story. Both Margaret Mitchell's novel and the 1939 classic film are about Scarlett O'Hara and Rhett Butler. What drives the movie is one central question: Will these two ever get together? So if you wish to do a story about the Civil War, you must write a specific story about specific people. Remember it is important not to confuse venue with what a story is really about. Your job as author is to find the story within the story.

Anthony Minghella, screenwriter and director of *The English Patient* and *The Talented Mr. Ripley*, in an interview published in *Written By*, the magazine of the screenwriters union, Writers Guild of America, says this:

> I'm most spurred on by the curiosity of what it means to be human. If the character is so distant from anybody that we know or understand, it's very hard to learn anything ... You feel right from the beginning that you do not inhabit the same journey that the character is going on ... I want to feel in film.

Frank Pierson, screenwriter of *Cool Hand Luke, Dog Day Afternoon,* and *A Star is Born*, says that a story starts by beginning with the characters and their needs and motives, then brings them together.

I can't resist a humorous anecdote here. A couple of years ago, I was asked to be a final judge for the Ojai Film Festival and Frank Pierson was a guest speaker at the Awards Banquet. We all sat together on the panel as the great cinematographer Conrad Hall was given a lifetime achievement award. His son, also a cinematographer, spoke first of the great cinematic moments attributed to his father, such as the opening of *Cool Hand Luke* which starred Paul Newman. In the early minutes of the film, there's a memorable shot of a prison guard standing in the piercing Southern sun, wearing large sunglasses. In the lens of the glasses, you see the reflection of a prison gang working on the road. It sets up the scene brilliantly. Hall's son went on to introduce Frank Pierson, who happened to receive an Oscar nomination for co-writing *Cool Hand Luke*. Pierson, a gentle and thoughtful man, rose and was about to speak his prepared speech before presenting the award to Connie Hall, sitting nearby on the raised platform. After a pause, however, Pierson smiled and said he couldn't help but mention that the now-famous scene at the beginning of *Cool Hand Luke* just referred to, was indeed beautifully photographed by Connie Hall — but first it was written in his script as stage directions! Laughter erupted, and a lovely moment transpired as Frank Pierson looked over at Connie Hall, who was also laughing by now. Not the first time that Hollywood forgets that in the beginning is the Word!

Once when I spoke at Sundance Film Festival where *Angel Passing* (with Hume Cronyn and Calista Flockhart) was being screened, someone commented on how little dialogue the film had. I was the co-writer of this film. She assumed that the writer only wrote the spoken words in a film. "No," I answered "a screenwriter writes not only the dialogue but the stage directions or what the actors do, as well as the setting of the scenes, mood, even the weather."

Often the most important writing is what is not said, but implied or shown. Quite often what the character does tells us more in a film than what he thinks or says. So once again, it begins and ends with character.

What is the main drive of the character? The following exercises will help delve into this more. Here's an exercise to serve as a pencil sketch for your character, using first a prototype from your own life.

EXERCISE

Pick a real-life character who most influenced you before the age of twenty-one. (Not Marilyn Monroe or James Dean, please!) Someone you knew personally. Now begin to visualize him/her and jot down what strikes you about this character. The following questions might help.

What are the physical attributes? Age, height, weight, handsome, fair?

What does he care about?

His greatest triumph?

His greatest failure?

His greatest obstacle?

His dream?

His greatest drive in life?

What does he like to remember from the past?

What does he like to forget?

What is his character flaw?

What is a visual image or metaphor to symbolize your character?

This might be an animal (*Raging Bull*), flower (*Steel Magnolias*), object (Rosebud the sled, as in *Citizen Kane*), a bird (*The Painted Bird*), gem (*The Bluest Eye*) or simply a color (*The Color Purple*).

All right, now write one page describing the person you have chosen from your own life. Try to focus on him/her and not just how you feel about the person. If I walked into a crowded room of two hundred people after reading what you have written, your character should stand out.

EXERCISE

Now just take a page and put the name of a character at the top. This can be an character in your existing story or someone you make up now.

Now, just look at the character's name and free associate. Start listing random traits, beginning with name, age, physical description. Don't bother writing complete sentences; one word for each will suffice. And it need not make any sense. Now move on to psychological traits and likes and dislikes. For instant, likes the color pink, always wears it. Smokes a corncob pipe. Suffers from asthma. Be as specific as possible.

This exercise serves to make your character real. It may even lead to scenes you had not thought of beforehand. By playfully jotting down random traits, some may not fit. Good. That's true in life as well. Now let's try another exercise to illustrate this very point.

EXERCISE

Create a back story for your main character.

Write a one-page biography which ends just before your story begins. Whether you incorporate all the details of the back story or not, it does not matter. What is important is that you will have a more three-dimensional character who has lived a life before he steps onto your page.

EXERCISE

My main character begins as _____ and ends as _____
_____. What lesson has he learned? How has he changed?

    This last one is an exercise designed to define the *character arc*. The best stories — though not all — have a major character which starts out at one place and ends up at quite another, the more extreme the better. In Hollywood, this is referred to as the arc. The currently successful book and film, *Seabiscuit*, set during the Depression in America is a good example. Three very different men survive hard knocks to come together in triumph at the end. The arc may go in the opposite direction. For example, *King Lear*, *Hamlet*, and *Macbeth* are other examples where three powerful men are reduced to death and tragedy through fatal character flaws. King Lear's suspicious nature, Hamlet's inability to act, and the ruthless ambition of Macbeth create marvelous character arcs resulting in extreme conclusions. Shakespeare knew his craft all right. That's one workshop I should like to have taken!

    Martin Luther remarked at the end of his life, "Now I know it is not that man in Rome that is the problem. It is that man in me." Every major character arc should provide a revelation at the end of the story. The journey of your story should arrive at a point where your character has learned some major lesson which changes him forever. Luke in *Star Wars* or Humphrey Bogart's Rick in *Casablanca* are but two examples as is Scarlett O'Hara in *Gone with the Wind*, who realizes she has really loved Rhett all along, only it is too late.

    Interestingly enough, *Forrest Gump* (novel and film) is an exception to this rule. Though everyone around Gump changes, he stays pretty much the same from beginning to end. The archetype of the dumpling (wise fool) from fairy tales works as well today as a few centuries ago. This archetype is very popular in American films from Jerry Lewis to Adam Sandler to Peter Sellers in *Being There*.

    Know your characters as well as you would a close friend or relative. This is one reason prototypes are helpful as a starting point. The attributes are real ones. Remember, however, to look for situations where their innermost feelings can be externalized into concrete outer action.

Action is character. What a person does is what he is, not what he says. This is why a good technique is to have your character say one thing and do the opposite. For instance when a villain says, "Trust me" — you cringe when you read or hear it. Character is mostly revealed not by what is said about him or even what he says about himself — but from his actions. Show, don't tell. Mother was right: actions speak louder than words!

Here's an exercise to practice going to emotional extremes.

EXERCISE: CHARACTER MONOLOGUE

Choose a main character in your story and write a first-person monologue. Let there be another person in the room with him, to whom he is speaking. Now let the situation be such that it brings out an extreme emotion from your speaking character: joy, despair, fear, anger, etc. Write one page of monologue in the first person from the character's point of view. The goal of this exercise is not to provide exposition as to plot but to push your character towards an extreme feeling. It need not make sense. Just go with it. What matters here is to *feel* the emotion, then write whatever comes out. Again, write whatever arises from the extreme feeling chosen.

It is not enough to write with one part of your brain. Equally valuable tools are a writer's emotions, memories, intuition, guts. It is so important to bring all of you to the table.

How to find your characters? Sometimes you might begin with a character based on someone you actually know, a prototype. Free yourself of stereotypes and other abstractions. Use prototypes. Family members or intimate friends are usually the first place to look for possible prototypes. Just remember to use fictional names! Or you may wish to write a composite of two or three persons you actually know by selecting various traits from separate individuals, then making a salad. In my first play, *On the Edge: The Final Years of Virginia Woolf,* I had two supporting male characters which in later drafts became one strong character, rather than two less interesting ones.

It also helps to love your character, to have enthusiasm for your character, as in *Harold and Maude, Auntie Mame, Norma Rae,* and *Driving Miss Daisy,* or Johnny Cash in *Walk the Line.* Remember, you must care for your character before an audience or reader will. If you have enthusiasm for him, that enthusiasm is contagious and will come off the page. Draw from your own past from those who inhabit your own life. Allow how you feel about them to pour into your characters and their story. When choosing characters which excite, often the story will follow, as in the plays of Tennessee Williams. He begins with Amanda, Tom, and Laura, and from this dysfunctional mother-son-daughter relationship, a great play emerges, *The Glass Menagerie.* It is his most autobiographical play and some say his best.

Apart from using prototypes from his own family (i.e., his sister Rose and his dominating mother), Williams imbues his strong feelings into every line in the play. He pours his heart onto the page, and it is truly a gift of himself to us. As an audience, we, in turn, feel through his characters, and through feeling, *catharsis* occurs. Webster's Dictionary defines catharsis as "a purifying release of the emotions or of tension through art." This is one reason why when one walks out of a great play, even a tragedy such as Shakespeare's *King Lear,* one does not feel sad but elated. Catharsis has taken place. I cannot admit to feeling the same with many films or books today. Why is this? What is often missing is the dimension of the main character. Modern characters too often lack the epic proportion which may serve as an archetypal container for transformation or catharsis to occur. As collective containers, they are simply too small.

Years ago when I was earning my living in New York as an actress, I had the good luck to play the title role in a play adaptation of Tolstoy's superb novel, *Anna Karenina.* It was adapted and directed by the great Russian actress, Eugenie Leontovich, who had earlier triumphed on Broadway in *Anastasia.* So I was playing the role of Anna in *Anna K,* which ran for nine months at the Actors Playhouse, eight shows a week, two shows a day on the weekends. After a performance, I would be so elated that I would need several hours to come down in order to sleep. This was also true when I played Juliet in the National Arts Theatre's production of *Romeo and Juliet*, also in New York. Yet — and here's the point — when I played major roles in contemporary plays, this was not the case. There, I could go straight home and go to sleep. It was far easier to shed the role and return to normal life. You see, I had not been lifted up to those ethereal regions where the gods play. It was a shorter distance to return to me. Perhaps this says something about our modern times. What is different? What has been lost?

Later I would sometimes — though not often — experience this as a writer, when I felt I had become the character I created, and that the character was having its way with me. A thrilling experience. You might say a kind of love affair.

> When I love writing the most is when a character takes over.
> — Robert Benton, screenwriter (*Bonnie and Clyde*, *Kramer vs. Kramer*, *Places in the Heart*)

Make a good impression. The first impression of your main character is crucial. Paul Newman knows this well. In his earlier films, at the height of his stardom, Newman would insist that each movie begin with him alone on screen in order to introduce the main "star" character. These scenes were often done without dialogue — written by the screenwriter — and would precede the opening credits. Check out *Cool Hand Luke* or *Harper*. So the audience would be first introduced to the personality of the main character before the story even began.

A more recent example is the pre-credit scene of Toby McGuire's *Spiderman* as he swoops from skyscraper to skyscraper, introducing who the main character is. Later concealed behind his nerd-like schoolboy persona, he says, "Who am I? You're sure you want to know?" The audience knows long before the other characters that this wimp is really *Spiderman*.

Though theme is important as discussed in the previous chapter, story is more than the plot or theme. It is the inner psychological state of the main character which fuels and drives the external plot.

> Plot is character.
> — Aristotle

Earlier we learned that all stories begin with a problem. And, of course, there has to be a *who* to have the problem. So the beginning of any story in any genre introduces a main character who has a problem. He wants something he cannot get because of some inner and/or outer obstacle. It is best to give him both an inner and outer obstacle.

> A novel is a meditation on existence, seen through imaginary characters.
> — Milan Kundera, author of *The Unbearable Lightness of Being*

STRUCTURING CHARACTERS

Consider a portrait painter who first draws a pencil sketch or cartoon of his subject, then erases and re-draws it many times before he picks up his oil brush. Structuring multi-dimensional characters is similar. Building or structuring characters entails the same process as re-writing the story outline earlier discussed.

This is one reason I prefer to complete a first draft before re-writing. It provides a sense of the whole, where my characters are going. Also it is much easier to work on developing a character once you have something on paper. As King Lear said, "Nothing comes from nothing."

Better to write something down than talk it over too much with friends or spouses. Just remember to keep your inner critic in the closet during these early explorations! The pencil sketch will never be perfect, it's not meant to be. It is merely a starting point. And, as we all know, the toughest part is starting!

ARCHETYPES VERSUS STEREOTYPES

A discussion of archetypes might be helpful at this point. What is an archetype? An archetype is more or less what a prototype is — a model for your character. Only an archetype is something more: a mythic prototype. Archetypes are lived by us daily — either consciously or unconsciously. If you can create a character which conveys a universal archetype, the collective will identify, and respond more deeply to your story.

Let's take one example in film and explore it in depth. In Larry McMurtry's novel and later the award-winning film, *Terms of Endearment*, you might see Aurora (Shirley McLaine) as Demeter, the overly protective mother of her daughter, Emma (Debra Winger) or Persephone. The film won five major Oscars: Best Film, Director, Screenplay, Supporting Actor, and Actress. So it pays to have a basic knowledge of myth and archetypes! (Pick up the small Edith Hamilton's *Greek Myths* for starters.)

The theme of *Terms of Endearment* would be obsessive mother love — certainly a universal existing from ancient Greece to today. Aurora uses motherhood as a defense against Eros (passion) by keeping sexual fulfillment far away. It is also about the fierceness of a mother's love for her only child who is dying of cancer. In the Greek myth, the goddess Demeter descends into the underworld where Persephone, her daughter, has been abducted by Hades. In the film, Aurora descends into the hell of a modern uncaring hospital to fight for her daughter's comfort. Now, what was the very thing Aurora avoided? Desire and passion, right? So guess who moves next door? Jack Nicholson (Garrett) is a modern-day Dionysus (pleasures of life) archetype or that of Eros (passion). The character arc for Garrett is achieved by Eros/Dionysus growing to a wider Agape (selfless) love, a love not merely sexual. Aurora, on the other hand, must open, allowing Eros (passion) into her life.

Aurora is all Mother, a primal Demeter. Motherhood is her sole identification. Ever since her daughter's birth, she has engaged in a symbiotic relationship with Emma (Persephone).

In this way, she has kept passion (Eros) safely removed from her well-ordered, controlled life. She tends her garden as she does her daughter, yet is missing the one thing needed in order to bring her to life: Eros. Eros, sent by the gods in the form of Garrett Breedlove (free love?), is a former astronaut who has literally dropped from the sky!

As Eros is the son of Hermes (Trickster) and Aphrodite (Love) in Greek mythology, similarly Garrett carries all these archetypes, with a little Dionysus thrown in for the fun of it. He is first heard (off-camera) in a cry of passion as he plunges into his swimming pool next door — separated by a long fence or barrier. On the other side lies Demeter's controlled world, a walled manicured garden, no room for the spontaneous; chaos and risk are not welcomed here. Garrett makes his Dionysian move drawing Aurora away from her walled world and bestowing the first touch of Eros, along with some Hermetic play. "You're toying with me," she says in disgust. Aurora is clearly not yet ready to welcome Eros into her life. Later in revolt at her fifty-something birthday party surrounded by non-sexual admirers, she is faced with a life passing by, without Eros. Instinctively, Aurora knows where to go to fulfill this need. Her first symbolic gesture is to remove her shoes as she approaches the temple of Eros, i.e., Garrett's house next door.

The first date sees an awkward Aphrodite (beauty) dressed in fluffy, feminine allure. As her persona cover or scarf blows away in the fast drive of passion, the first semblance of control is hermetically stolen away, the unraveling begins, with a little Dionysian bourbon and vulgarism thrown in. Later the same night Demeter calls on Aphrodite, then summons the courage to invite Eros to her bedroom to see her etchings, i.e., her Renoir painting. In an interesting ironic twist, the painting resembles her young daughter, now grown up and away, living in Iowa. Later on, we find Demeter very much alive as she rages in the underworld of a cancer ward where Emma (Persephone) lays dying. There is no force like a mother's wrath. At the end, Emma gives a piercing last look at the mother who was never satisfied with her. In this gaze we witness the strongest love: that of a mother for her child. Here Aurora must release Emma to the underworld of death. There will be no spring visitations for this Persephone. There is nothing harder than this letting go of a mother's love. Plato said that Eros is the one who gives souls strength to ascend to heaven after death. Garrett, as Eros, saves Aurora when her life as Demeter ends with Emma's death. Thus Aurora, whose very name means dawn, invites Aphrodite's son, Eros, into a new life, where she will raise Emma's children with his help. Eros (Garrett) himself is now tamed by an awakening of agape love, a love not limited to sex. With him, a more balanced Demeter will mother again, yet this time embracing both Aphrodite and Eros.

As you see, a little mythology goes a long way in creating multi-dimensional characters. The Greeks had a phenomenal insight into human nature. They learned about psychology by listening to the stories of their myths and archetypes, or by watching the great plays of Euripides, Sophocles, and Aristophanes. Psychologists came later. Deep inside our souls is Eros, a life force of energy of passion. There is no greater rule of success than to tap the collective archetypes at the right time.

A word on mythology. Myths are stories which mirror man's search for meaning. A myth is the universal experience of being human. There is no right interpretation of myth — no dogmas here as in religion. A civilization requires a myth in order to live.

Myth is how we make sense in a senseless world.
— Rollo May

EXERCISE

Read a story from the Greek or Roman myths. Keep your mind open and see who pops up. Perhaps a Dionysian uncle who was a little too much in his cups or an Artemis tomboy more at home in the forest than a house with people. You have found your prototype. Read the myth again and see what visual images pop up from your unconscious. Let them arise by themselves — don't try too hard. This works best with effortless striving. Next, work with whatever visual image arises and write a monologue from his/her point of view. Or a dialogue between two archetypes who are opposites, as were Demeter and Eros (MacLaine and Nicholson) in the previous example.

Sometimes a character must be born and be given time to grow in your unconscious before finding his way onto the page. When you carry the archetypal image, you may be surprised when you meet it in the external world. You might perhaps unexpectedly glimpse the Artemis tomboy in the grocery store — someone who represents the exact physical image you need for your character, yet to be born. The writing process can be magical, if you give yourself to it.

EXERCISE

Using the same character image discovered in the previous exercise, find the foremost desire of your main character and you are on your way to developing your plot and story. Just ask the image: What do you want more than anything else? What stands in your way?

It is desire that shapes destiny. Desire is the first step in building story structure. Action is character: what a person does is what he is, not what he says. Choice is character. Why does a person choose this person to love or to hate?

EXERCISE

Write a dialogue illustrating what your character believes or voices as a belief when contrasted by his actions. Let the other character in the dialogue face him with the lie.

> Man is what he believes.
> — Anton Chekhov

Characters evolve when little by little, page by page, the lies are stripped away. See, for example, Ingmar Bergman's film *Autumn Sonata*. This dismantling of lies provides the dramatic action for the story. Always remember, however, that what is essential in any story is not plot, not what happens, but rather how what happens acts upon and changes your main character for better or worse, and subsequently how what happens alters his relationships with himself and his world.

> See relationship as the place where soul works out its destiny.
> — Thomas Moore

This kind of writing is the work of soul. It provides the reader and audience (as well as the writer) with a mirror into their souls. In this way, you can provide meaning to the task of living. By providing universal characters, you, as the writer, offer a safe container for others to discover themselves. And this, as much as anything else, is an act of love.

Love is what life is about, really, deep, deep inside ... You're always trying to find yourself in other people. You're trying to find a mirror of yourself.
    — Bille August, Danish film director (*The House of the Spirits*)

A word of caution here though. This must not be a polemic or message, but executed through character. *Show, don't tell.* Specifics are essential. In the specific lies the universal and not the other way round.

I'd like to end this chapter on Character with an example from one of the finest novels ever written in English: *Middlemarch* by George Eliot, written in the nineteenth century. The best of stories usually will have a human being whose life is out of balance in pursuit of something to restore that balance. In the character of Dorothea, there is a tremendous sense of guilt at being born a gentlewoman in nineteenth-century England, and not doing anything important. Dorothea yearns to make the world a better place. This desire drives her to accept an offer of marriage to a cruel and unfeeling man. She will serve his supposed great work — later revealed to be a sham. However, her unselfish drive persists, and eventually she overcomes her trials and does indeed make the world a better place, finding in the end her own happiness as well. Notice the warmth of feeling Eliot has for her main character.

Her full nature spent itself in deeds which left no great name upon the earth, but the effect of her being on those around her was incalculable. For the growing good of the world is partly dependent on unhistoric acts and on all those Dorotheas who lived faithfully their hidden lives and rest contentedly in unvisited tombs.
    — George Eliot, *Middlemarch*

Characters do not exist in a vacuum — except maybe for Samuel Beckett's characters. Characters exist in relationship and in conflict with other characters. Time spent on developing character will not be wasted. Time spent developing your story through the drives of your main characters will provide the central key to any great story. Tell me what a man longs for, and I will show you who he is.

Once you know your characters, you must allow them to speak in their own voices. So let us next explore the secret of writing stunning dialogue.

Chapter 6

The Secret of Writing Stunning Dialogue

Who the hell wants to hear actors speak?
— Harry Warner (Warner Brothers, 1927)

*W*ELL, TIMES CHANGE. In 1927, few thought it possible that silent films would not continue forever. Even Charlie Chaplin delayed adding words to his films as long as possible. He said having the little tramp speak would be as absurd as if the ballet dancer, Nijinsky, stopped dancing and suddenly talked! He thought it would destroy the magic. Nonetheless, dialogue came, and Hollywood films have been talking ever since. Even so, it should be remembered that often the most memorable part of any play or film is not what is said, but the silent moments before, after, and especially between the lines. Usually these are the moments remembered when we think of our favorite films — not the dialogue. Ursula K. Le Guin (*The Earthsea Trilogy*) once remarked that "The artist deals with what cannot be said in words. The novelist says in words what cannot be said in words."

> Do not the most moving moments of our lives find us all without words?
> — Marcel Marceau

During my New York acting years, I was invited to a small gathering on Central Park West for a party where the French mime, Marcel Marceau, was invited after his nightly successful Broadway one-man show. An unforgettable evening was to follow. At one point, in my friend's living room overlooking Central Park, Marceau stood up and spontaneously began to perform his famous mime of catching a butterfly — without make-up or costume. I was spellbound, realizing that without the traditional white face of a clown, it was all the more poignant. Naked. Vulnerable. Simplicity was the key. Then a kind of epiphany occurred with crystal clarity. This was not about a man chasing a butterfly, but human beings trying to capture Life. How vulnerable we are in this persistent pursuit.

The most important person in any painting is the light.
— Edouard Manet

Similarly, the most important part of any play or film is the silence or subtext. Hence, the most important aspect of dialogue is what is not said but what is implied or felt. As a playwright and screen-writer, I learned that the dramatic action of the story lives in the subtext: the unsaid. Though words are needed to point to the silence, they are only pointers.

In novels, or biographies and memoirs as well, the words serve to carry the reader to the silent moment when he is moved. In *Wuthering Heights,* Catherine, who is unable to separate from Heathcliff, cries out, "Heathcliff. I am Heathcliff." Again, silence while the reader experiences exactly what Emily Bronte intended. Anyone who has ever truly loved will understand this identification with the beloved.

So subtext — below the text — is where it's at. Subtext is what is implied but never explicitly said. A comic example of subtext is seen in Woody Allen's film, *Annie Hall*, which brought home four Oscars. Woody Allen is trying to impress Diane Keaton (Annie), whom he has just met. They speak banal sophisticated dialogue trying to impress the other, while the subtext or what they are really thinking is shown as subtitles. A few examples are "She must think I'm a jerk" or "I can't believe I said that." "He must think

I'm dumb." Here is a hilarious example of subtext. Not what we say (text) but what we are really thinking and feeling (subtext).

It is often said that fiction is about what happens inside people, whereas plays or films are about what happens between people. However, with the strong influence of television and film today, novels and nonfiction narratives are written with more and more dialogue as well as more visual writing generally associated with screenplays. So when examples are given from films or plays, please note that it applies today to all narrative or story forms.

The word dialogue comes from the Greek dia (through) and logos (word). Hence the very meaning of dialogue is through words. Another way of saying this is that words hint at what you are trying to say in your story. *Not the thing in itself.* This said, I should add, that if it is necessary to plainly state the theme of your story, this is best served at the conclusion. "It is a far, far better thing I do today than I have ever done before," writes Charles Dickens in *A Tale of Two Cities*, as his character is about to sacrifice his life for that of a better man, thereby redeeming all his past less noble acts.

Wait as long as possible to say what must be said, is crying out to be said, and only then say it. Think of good writing as foreplay, waiting as long as possible for the thrust of theme. This increases the power of a well-told story.

Dialogue then is merely the tip of the iceberg. It's what is going on beneath the lines that really matters. Writing plays and screenplays, I learned that what is real in the script is what is not said. The dramatic action of the story lives in the subtext, the unsaid. It is pointed to, though preferably never explicitly stated until the end

Soul is a bit like this. You cannot hold it in your hand — yet it is real. You cannot define soul — only point to it. You may feel it with your whole being as in peak experiences in life, but try to claim it as your own, and you quickly discover how illusive the Real can be. It can be felt, experienced, but never owned. The best stories point to what you feel when you're reading them, the most important parts not explicitly spelled out. So good writing is about what is not said.

It is well and good to have a good ear as a writer. Often you will overhear a bit of dialogue that is perfect for one of your characters. Yet if your characters are just talking, making conversation, you're in trouble.

Often students would bring in a dialogue exercise which I would then critique. Invariably, the student would protest by saying, "But that's exactly what they said!" Then I would remind him that dialogue is not conversation. Get this? Dialogue is not conversation. The difference is that dialogue must serve two functions. The functions of dialogue are to:

1) Reveal character.
2) Move the plot forward.

If your lines do neither of these, they are generally the ones to drop on the next re-write. This is so even if they are your favorite lines in the whole piece — especially if they are your favorite lines in the whole piece! Re-writing is a ruthless and necessary part of the writing process. However, it is important to remember how vitally important it is to risk all when writing the first draft, without that inner critic on your shoulder. Let it flow — you can always cut later. And it's much easier to cut than to add. Gradually, through the practice of writing, you will instinctively know which lines ring true and which false. Listen to that inner guide. It is usually spot on.

> Failure is part of the creative process. If you're afraid of it, you can't really create.
> — Danny DeVito, actor/producer

To continue with subtext, a picture is worth a thousand words, so here are two examples from Oscar-winning pictures. First, *Ordinary People*, Alvin Sargent's superb film adaptation of the novel by Judith Guest, directed by Robert Redford. Both Redford and Sargent won Oscars for this one.

The Story: A boating accident with two brothers. The mother's favorite son drowns while the lesser son lives. He knows that his mother loved his brother more and secretly wishes that he had died instead. Though nothing is explicitly said, it is clearly implied ... felt.

The Scene: This is the camera scene with Donald Sutherland, Mary Tyler Moore, and Timothy Hutton who plays their guilt-ridden son. It is a typical family scene with Donald Sutherland, the father, getting everyone together to take a family photo — an ordinary event for seemingly ordinary people. The dance goes on until the father realizes he doesn't have a picture with just mother and son, so he tries to organize one. The mother (Mary Tyler Moore) is uncomfortable standing next to the son who survived, thus making the son (Timothy Hutton) feel unwanted. The awkwardness increases as Moore continues to protest by insisting that she take another photo of the two of them again until Hutton explodes and says what has been subtext for the last five minutes: "Goddamn it! Don't you see? She doesn't want a picture with me!" The truth is out. Good writing. Good film.

Here's another Oscar-winning example, *Kramer vs. Kramer*. Robert Benton adapted the novel by Avery Corman and also directed this film which garnered five Oscars.

The Story: Wife walks out on workaholic husband, leaving him to take care of their young son.

The Scene: Dustin Hoffman is making French toast for Justin Henry, his five-year-old son whose mother, Meryl Streep, has just deserted them. Hoffman tries to pretend nothing is wrong and make his son breakfast — which he has never done before. He doesn't really know how to make French toast and keeps getting it wrong until he finally blows and says "Damn her!" The little boy has felt the subtext all along but not until it actually bursts forth and he hears his mother referred to does it really go home. His mother has left them. The truth is out. Good writing. Good film.

Here's another example, from *The Queen* (2006) which stars Helen Mirren.

The Story explores the repressed monarch during the week of Princess Diana's tragic and sudden death. Conditioned to conceal her feelings behind the mask of monarch, she is undergoing tremendous pressure as her people criticize her for not showing feeling over Diana's death — even though Diana is no longer part of the royal family.

The Scene: Elizabeth is stoic throughout except for a moment alone in her country place, Balfour, when her jeep breaks down in the middle of a rushing stream. She gets out of the car, and spies a lone stag standing majestically nearby. Queen Elizabeth weeps, then hearing the approaching hunters, quickly shoos the noble beast away. Good writing. Good film.

In early drafts, the dialogue might be explicit. For instance, one character might say I hate you or I love you, or I am afraid, has my mother left us? Then the task is in later drafts to write in such a way that your audience or reader first feels the subtext, without actually being told. To delay the telling as long as possible, until it cannot be contained a moment longer, and unexpectedly bursts forth. This is much stronger than saying too much from the start. Remember we read and view films in order to feel something. Words — though important — are simply pointers to what is really going on between the characters or within the main character.

A memorable final scene can be viewed (or read) in John Galsworthy's novel, *The Forsyte Saga: To Let* and the second, excellent television adaptation (Masterpiece Theatre for National Public Television). It is Soames' last meeting with his former wife, Ireni, whom he still loves. At a previous meeting, years after their divorce, he became violent and Ireni told him to leave, refusing to even shake his hand. In the later scene, he graciously takes his leave and is surprised when Ireni calls him back.

IRENI

Wait. Please wait.

Ireni now offers her hand to say goodbye. Soames returns to her, and clumsily, hastily removes his right glove before shaking hands. Then he looks at her, without bitterness.

SOAMES

I won't see you again.

IRENI

(without fear or bitterness)

Probably not.

They remain holding their hands for another prolonged moment, and she smiles a tender smile which he is able at last to receive. Then he walks away. Resolution at last.

The brilliance here is having Soames remove his leather glove before shaking hands with the woman he lost, the woman he had been unable to see as more than a possession. Here the scant dialogue dissolves leaving you with the moment between the characters, an image which remains long after the final credits of the film.

It is often more interesting when there is a gap or contradiction between what a character is saying and what he or she is doing, as in the preceding examples. It is the gap that makes us feel the chill on our neck. What a character does is who he is — not what he says. One Oscar-winning example is *Unforgiven* when the ruthless gunfighter of yesterday played by Clint Eastwood says, "I'm not like that anymore." Later it is discovered by his actions that he remains the ruthless gunfighter he always was.

So, the most important part of a play or film is what is not said. Subtext: what lives in-between the lines of your text or below the text. Take the death scene in *Lonesome Dove*, the television miniseries adapted from Larry McMurtry's novel set in the American West, starring Tommy Lee Jones and Robert Duvall.

The Story: This is a riveting story of two tough Texas Rangers who have been together for decades making the American West a safer place.

The Scene: Robert Duvall is dying and Jones has been searching for him. He finally tracks him down, only to learn from the sawbones (doctor) that it is too late. His friend will soon die. Then there follows a beautifully written scene by Texas screenwriter, Bill Whittliff. There can be no doubt of the deep love these two friends have for one another, even though neither speaks of love outright. Taken on the surface, the spoken lines seem to be sparring as the characters have always done, "No wonder women never liked you, Woodrow." or "You never do a day's work anyway." However, the subtext rings loud and clear: You are my dearest friend in all the world and I don't want you to die. Here is an excellent example of a character-driven drama with stunning, authentic dialogue throughout.

I am reminded of a script meeting I had with HBO executives and my director, David Jones (no relation), for my first movie, *The Christmas Wife*. Script meetings in Hollywood usually mean a forum where those who don't write tell the writer how to write. In this particular meeting, two of the executives suggested three or four things that I should add to my script. I sat there not knowing what to say and looked forlornly at my more experienced British director, David Jones. David then said to the producers, "Actually all of those elements are in Catherine's script, only they're subtext." Of course, to satisfy Hollywood, the result was an added scene (the poker-playing scene) where someone blatantly says to Jason Robards, whose wife has recently died, "It must be lonely for you now." What Uta Hagen, my acting teacher, would say to avoid: what is on the nose or obvious. And in teaching, I would say, "Show don't tell. And if you show, don't be redundant and tell." That said, however, I was fortunate that this was the only revision demanded for this film. After all, I was allowed to forego a sentimental wrap-up happy ending, something rare in Hollywood — especially for a Christmas movie!

In New York City, I taught playwriting for seven years at The New School University. When the chairman first called to invite me to teach, I said, "Writing can't be taught." He very cleverly replied, "Then teach it from that perspective." I was hooked, impressed that here was an academic institution which characteristically invited those who *do* to teach: professionals as well as academics. Here began my commitment to teach writing from a professional writer's perspective, and not mere theory. I called the class *The Writing-on-Your-Feet Playwriting Workshop* and used improvisations to teach the basic principles of playwriting. Why? Because I found that playwrights who did not have previous acting experience were often at a disadvantage when it came to dramatic writing. Through improvisations, I could sometimes trick the writers into writing with all of themselves: physically, emotionally, intuitively, and mentally. In an improvisation, you don't know what you will say until you say it. Hence, it is spontaneous, real, and often comes from an unexpected visceral and deeper part of your self.

Dramatic writing is quite different from writing books, where words are meant to be read. Plays or films are heard, seen, and felt

— not generally read. You cannot go back and have a second look as one does while reading a novel or story. The words are gone with the wind. Dramatic writing lives in the moment — rather like life. Also, what people say is quite different from a book of an author's or character's thoughts. So it is best to keep your characters complex and your words and dialogue simple, if writing plays and films. By this I don't mean shallow — just simple, short words rather than four syllable words that send one running to the dictionary. Dialogue should seem real whether spoken by a god, fairy, or plumber.

Each time I complete a first draft of a new play, the first thing I do is to invite fellow actors over for an evening to read the play aloud. I also invite three or four friends for their feedback — as well as to provide an audience for the actors. This process is both frightening and exciting. Frightening because it is difficult to know when you are so close to a new work if it is good or bad. Exciting because it is new and the juices are still flowing. I make sure never to read myself, but always to listen, with notepad in hand. It's also a good idea to tape record the reading so you can hear it again later. In any case, what is important is to hear the lines and watch the actors as they speak them. Are they natural? Authentic? Do they move the story? Reveal character? Is what I am trying to say clear? This is not a logical process. There are no graphs to show you statistically what dialogue works and what doesn't. You will simply feel it. Call it intuitive knowing, if you like. Also when an actor trips over a line or re-phrases it, that can be an important clue as to what to cut or rewrite. Sometimes an actor's re-wording is better than what you wrote in the first place. Actors are the most generous people I know, and are usually happy when you incorporate their impromptu re-phrasing of your line.

After hearing the early draft read aloud with a few chosen friends, I return to the desk and begin the inevitable process of rewriting. As novels and short stories are also storytelling, I wonder if this hearing it read aloud would not be a good idea for all narrative works, as well as plays and screenplays. It serves to encourage a flow to the story.

Reading aloud to one another has become a lost art. Even reading a book to one's self may one day become lost in this age of silicon. Now children watch television or computer games. One of my favorite quality times with my son, Christopher, was reading bedtime stories. Later when he got older, we continued, each taking turns reading aloud the novels of Dickens or short stories. Today, it might be fun for parents and children or friends to read the *Harry Potter* novels to each other... before they see the film. In any case, wouldn't it be grand to foster the love of story in all ages?

Another tip is to vary the rhythm of dialogue. That is, intersperse long sentences with short staccato ones. Different characters speak in different rhythms. Find the rhythm suitable for each character. Even visually, a page of dialogue should have variation.

In 1939, when Rhett Butler said, "Frankly, my dear, I don't give a damn," American audiences were dazzled. Such language had not been heard on film before then. Today one is blunted with profanity, and in the end, like gratuitous sex, I think it is less effective than one well-placed four-letter word or erotic suggestion. The same may be said of gratuitous violence in today's media, and here I include news coverage as well. And yet we puzzle over the escalation of violence in our country. Though in a minority, I have remained committed to socially responsible writing, that is, films and plays without gratuitous sex or violence.

Dialogue at its best should be used as an extension of character. There is no separation between the character of Rhett Butler and his dialogue or Scarlett and her hot-tempered words. The challenge of dramatic writing is to find the voice for each character so that it won't sound like one voice — that of the writer. Dustin Hoffman in *Kramer vs. Kramer* asks his five-year-old son, Justin Henry, what time it is, and young Henry replies, "The little hand is on the seven and the big one on the twelve." This dialogue rings true. That is exactly how a five-year-old speaks.

As the key to writing great stories is creating great characters, so is the secret to writing stunning dialogue linked to character. I tell my students and clients that if I read a page of dialogue with the characters names removed, I should be able to tell who said what. In other words, each character must speak in an individual manner, in contrast from other characters in your story.

One delightful example is the character of Poirot, the Belgian sleuth, from the Agatha Christie *Poirot* mysteries. It is useful to remember that before the *Harry Potter* books, Christie's mystery novels sold more than any other books, other than the Bible! Poirot is set apart as a character by the manner in which he speaks his dialogue. Though extremely intelligent, he never quite achieves a command of the English language, and manages to alter one word every time he attempts a commonplace English saying. Here's an example. Instead of saying "I put my foot in my mouth," Poirot would say "I put the toe in the mouth." Funny. This device is called a malapropism or ludicrous misuse of a word. The word is taken from the character of Mrs. Malaprop in Sheridan's eighteenth-century play, *The Rivals*. And two hundred years later, it still works every time!

Another key to writing stunning dialogue is to research the vocation of your character. For instance, a baseball player might refer to being in love and say, "I feel like I'm on a hitting streak that never ends!" A dentist might notice someone's smile. A jazz musician might use a metaphor of playing it as it comes. And so on.

Know your characters well enough to know how they think and speak. That is not only their vocation, but their economic and social background, nationality, time period, and other aspects that create a personality. When you go deep enough, layer by layer, each and every character is unique.

In the Oscar-winning biographical film, *A Beautiful Mind*, written by Akiva Goldsman and starring Russell Crowe as John Forbes Nash, Jr., the Nobel Laureate mathematician says, "Perhaps it is good to have a beautiful mind, but an even greater gift is to discover a beautiful heart."

Another way to view writing dialogue is a search for meaning. What is the meaning you are trying to convey with your story? Meaning is collective, yet language is specific. We rely on language or speech to communicate, but at best, words can only suggest meaning.

In an interview with Mark Seal for *American Way*, Pulitzer Prize–winning playwright Horton Foote discusses the meaning of his plays and films. Foote won the Oscar for his beautiful screenplay, *Tender Mercies,* which won Robert Duvall an Oscar, as well. He also wrote *The Trip to Bountiful* which earned the inimitable Geraldine Page an Oscar. The interviewer pointed out that it had been said that in his work he seemed to be trying to define the meaning of "home." Foote replied that "Well, I've been told that so many times that I finally felt that, well, yes, maybe I am trying to define the meaning of 'home.' You don't always consciously know what you're doing. Obviously, I'm attracted to this idea of trying to define what 'home' is."

You may not consciously know what the story's theme is until you have a first draft written. Knowing what it is eventually can be very helpful in guiding re-writes in order to better focus the theme as well as structure your story.

At first, the lines may be far from revealing your theme or what your story is about, but then as the story and characters develop, what they say gets closer and closer to your theme. Then at the climax or near the end of their story, the theme is bluntly stated or arises from some revelation your main character undergoes. Yet all along, the main character is searching for something he knows only unconsciously. You might want to refer back to Chapter 2: Seven Steps to Story Structure. The Problem of the story (step 1) will concern the main character's need which is distinctly different from desire (step 2). The main character will not become aware of his need until the end. Gradually, the lies are stripped away, the obstacles removed one by one until he stands naked before the truth.

A useful technique to convey necessary exposition and back story is the dialogue spoken by the supporting characters. It is generally best to have your supporting characters reveal your main character's back story. By back story, I mean his life before your story begins, yet which somehow affects what is happening to him now. By exposition, I mean the set ups for place and plot. Shakespeare used servants or soldiers to provide the necessary information that would be needed later to understand what Hamlet or Othello was doing.

EAVESDROPPING DIALOGUE EXERCISE

Remember one line you have overheard recently. Perhaps you overheard it in a store or at home with your family or friends, or anywhere. Take the one line and write a two-page dialogue around it with two characters. You need not know the original context of the overheard line, in fact, it is better if you don't. Just make up the situation and characters, appropriating the one line.

2 + 1 DIALOGUE EXERCISE

Write a dialogue between two characters. The purpose here is to reveal character by showing three traits, the third one seeming not to fit with the first two. For example, Andy Sipowicz, the hardened cop on *NYPD Blue,* is an alcoholic racist who raises tropical fish.

MONOLOGUE AND SOLILOQUY

Soliloquy comes from the Latin solus (alone) plus loqui (to speak). So it means to speak to one's self. A well-known example of soliloquy is Shakespeare's *Hamlet*: "To be or not to be" where Hamlet is alone on stage, thinking to himself out loud.

Monologue comes from the Greek *monos* (one) plus *logos* (speech) and means one long speech. The two functions of dialogue apply here as well. That is, to reveal character and/or push the plot forward. Here is an example of using monologue to describe the main character's inner life.

August Strindberg uses monologue to reveal the title character in his play, *Miss Julie* when she is telling John, her servant and soon to be lover, how she feels. Miss Julie is an aristocrat who fancies her lower-class servant, a taboo. Her conflict is following her heart, though knowing that to do so, would bring her down.

John has just said to her, "You are strange, you know."

Julie replies:

Perhaps I am, but so are you. Besides, everything is strange. Life, men, the whole thing is simply an iceberg which is driven out on the water until it sinks — sinks. I have a dream which comes up now and again, and now it haunts me. I am sitting on the top of a high pillar and can't see any possibility of getting down; I feel dizzy when I look down, but I have to get down all the same. I haven't got the pluck to throw myself off. I can't keep my balance and I want to fall over, but I don't fall. And I don't get a moment's peace until I'm down below. No rest until I've got to the ground, and when I've got down to the ground, I want to get right into the earth. Have you ever felt anything like that?

Metaphor is a figure of speech depicting an object which implicitly represents something else. When Julie speaks of sitting on the top of a high pillar and looking down, the playwright, Strindberg, is using metaphor to describe her inner conflict of belonging to the upper class while desiring a man from the lower class, her own servant.

When Julie says, "and when I've got down to the ground, I want to get right into the earth," she implies that she wants to make love to her servant, John.

Monologue can sometimes allow the character to reveal their back story, what occurred before the story begins. Here's an example from Pulitzer Prize–winning playwright August Wilson's *Joe Turner's Come and Gone*. Loomis has just returned from working on a chain gang and is searching for his wife and child. The play speaks of the residue of slavery in America. (Notice also the use of wrong grammar to depict the character's social and economic background.) Here the character, Loomis, reveals his soul:

My wife Martha gone from me after Joe Turner catched me. Got out from under Joe Turner on his birthday. Me and forty other men put in our seven years and he let us go on his birthday. I made it back to Henry Thompson's place where me and Martha was sharecropping and Martha's gone. She taken my little girl and left her with her mama and took off North. We been looking for her ever since. That's been going on four years now we been looking. That's the only thing I know to do. I just wanna see her face so I can get me a starting place in the world. The world got to start somewhere. That's what I been looking for. I been wandering a long time in somebody else's world. When I find my wife that be the making of my own.

Observe here the rhythm and music in the playwright's lyrical portrayal of a relatively simple character.

Monologue is just as effective in novels, biographies, or political speeches.

Consider the "I Have a Dream" speech of Martin Luther King. Note the repetition of "I have a dream" which emotionally works on the audience. The words are used to make us feel.

Often the monologue is used by the author to put forth his theme, why he wrote the novel in the first place. This is usually placed towards the end of the story. John Steinbeck's monologue in *The Grapes of Wrath,* spoken with simple eloquence by Henry Fonda in John Ford's 1940 film adaptation, is one such example. Steinbeck's opus was published in 1939 but still sings eloquently of the poor man's struggle in an America ruled by the rich. Steinbeck, who won the Nobel Prize in 1962, was writing about the Depression in America and the bitter strikes in California fruit farms. Here are the words of Tom Joad, the story's protagonist, as he bids farewell to his mother. Tom's mother (Jane Darwell) asks him, "How'm I gonna know 'bout you? They might kill ya an' I wouldn't know. How'm I gonna know?"

                    TOM

Well, maybe like Casey says, a fella ain't got a soul of his own, but only a piece of a big one — an' then —

                    MA

Then what, Tom?

                    TOM

Then it don' matter. Then I'll be all aroun' in the dark. I'll be ever'where — wherever you look. Wherever there's a fight so hungry people can eat, I'll be there. Whenever there's a cop beatin' up a guy, I'll be there... I'll be in the way guys yell when they're mad... And when the people are eatin' the stuff they raise and living in the houses they build, I'll be there, too.

Then in the final scene, after Tom leaves and when Ma and Pa and the family are on the road again, Steinbeck clearly states the theme of his fine novel. Pa says, "We sure have taken a beating." Ma replies:

MA

```
We sure have, but we keep a comin'. We're the
people that live. They can't wipe us out. They can't
lick us. We'll go on forever, Pa, because we're the
people.
```

Notice that the writer waits until the very end to state his theme, after we have journeyed with the characters and been emotionally moved by their plight. *The Grapes of Wrath* was published in 1939. John Steinbeck was writing about the Depression in America — a specific time and a specific people — yet today in the age of corporate America, it is as universally true now as then. To reach the universal, find the specific.

As shown above, monologue can provide a window into the soul of your character and allow the reader or audience to feel what the character is feeling. Then the reader or audience identifies with the character and enters the character's world from within — through feeling.

Sometimes a novel or play will be exclusively monologue as in the play, *Vagina Monologues*, or some of the works of Nobel Laureate Samuel Beckett. The Swedish filmmaker, Ingmar Bergman, is a master of monologue as he explores the anguish depths of his characters in films such as *Persona*, *The Seventh Seal*, *Through a Glass Darkly*, or *Saraband*.

In *Winter Light*, Jonas, a fisherman, comes to Tomas, the village priest, seeking help. However, Tomas, the priest, is caught up in his own inner crisis, and inflicts his doubt and despair upon Jonas. Throughout the priest's monologue, Jonas simply listens, from his own despair. Having another character present even if they remain silent, adds a dimension of dramatic action. It adds relationship. The following is a brief excerpt from the three-page monologue from Bergman's film, *Winter Light*:

TOMAS

Jonas, listen to me a moment. I'll speak openly to
you, without reservations. You know my wife died
four years ago. I loved her. My life was at an end,
I'm not frightened of death, there isn't the least
reason for me to go on living… Believe me, I had
great dreams once. I was going to make my mark
in the world… Please, you must understand. I'm no
good as a clergyman. I chose my calling because
my mother and father were religious, pious, in a
deep and natural way. Maybe I didn't really love
them, but I wanted to please them. So I became
a clergyman and believed in God. (Gives a short
laugh.) An improbable, entirely private, fatherly
god. Who loved mankind, of course, but most of
all me. (Tomas is overcome by a violent attack of
coughing and has to get up. He draws a deep breath,
grimaces.)

Tomas is unable to even see Jonas, who after listening to three
more pages of Tomas's narcissistic monologue, quietly leaves, then
kills himself.

Here Bergman uses the monologue for background exposition of why Tomas became a clergyman in the first place. And the
speech also serves as a set up for what happens later, that is, Jonas's
suicide and Tomas's guilt over not being able to comfort one of
his parish.

The monologue is used to great advantage when you wish your
leading character to express what is deepest in him — when he is
speaking from his very soul.

A brilliant, more contemporary example is the final episode
of *Six Feet Under*, where Clare, the daughter, in voice over shares
with us how and when her various family members will die, in a
flash-forward.

In my play, *On the Edge: The Final Years of Virginia Woolf,* there is
a scene in Act II between Virginia and Vita, her close friend. Virginia
is on the verge of another nervous breakdown, and a concerned Vita
asks her, "How are you? I mean, how are you really?"

VIRGINIA

On the edge, I'm afraid. The strain, I think
of inhabiting two very different worlds. This
afternoon, for instance, when I was on my walk.
At first, I felt the wet grass on my feet. I saw
the green of the meadow, the Queen's lace, the
hollyhocks, and perhaps a robin sang. But then, I
began to be drawn into my novel. The more it drew
me, the less touch I had with the concrete world.
Do you understand, Vita? I was in another universe
entirely. I was in myself. And this world seemed
far, far more real than the one I had left.

VITA

That's where you really live, isn't it, darling?

VIRGINIA

As much as I dare. Sometimes, I think, one day I
may go too far and I shan't be able to find my
way back. And yet, despite the danger — or perhaps
because of it — something urges me on… deeper and
deeper. Half the time, I feel I'm on the brink of
some discovery, some extraordinary truth hitherto
unknown. Oh, Vita, how little we really know. There
must be another life. Not in dreams, but here
and now, with living people. I feel as if I was
standing on the edge of a precipice with my hair
blown back as if I were about to grasp something
that just evaded me. There must be another life.
This is too short, too broken. We know nothing,
even about ourselves. We're only just beginning to
understand.

(The music stops playing. Silence.)

Note that in this example, I had Vita ask another question in
the middle of what would have been a very long monologue. This
way it gives continuity to the relationship of the two characters on
stage. In Virginia's monologue she reveals her soul, that part of her
which is deeper than ordinary life. It also allows the audience to

enter that otherwise hidden world. Individual characters in both fiction and nonfiction serve as mirrors for the collective. Hence, the reader or audience is able to perceive something within which might otherwise be hidden.

Monologue is a powerful device when writing memoir or auto-biography. *The Journals* of Anais Nin's are a good example. Here is a window into what one woman feels at her mother's death:

> The pain deeper than at my father's death. I didn't love her enough.... While she was alive, she threatened my aspiration to escape the servitudes of women. Very early I was determined not to be like her but like the women who had enchanted and seduced my father, the mistresses who lured him away from us. When did I first feel this?... When she died, I remembered only her courage....

Nothing is more useful than a monologue to express the feelings of your character. A monologue allows the time and space for your character to demonstrate extreme feeling.

EMOTIONAL MONOLOGUE EXERCISE

The purpose of this monologue will be to reveal an extreme emotion in your character. Exposition does not matter here, only the feeling. It may be any feeling, negative or positive. Anger, jealousy, sexual excitement, etc. Just identify with the feeling and start writing. It is best to direct the monologue to another character in the scene. Write one page — no more than two. See how far you can push this to the extreme of whatever feeling you choose.

Monologue reveals the soul of your character, even their philosophy of life. Politicians use this form a lot. It is a powerful way to speak directly, intimately to their audience. A good example would be Nelson Mandela's 1994 Inaugural Speech in South Africa. Anyone who reads the following words can have no doubt about Mandela's philosophy.

> Our deepest fear is not that we are inadequate.

> Our deepest fear is that we are powerful beyond measure.

It is our Light, not our Darkness, that most frightens us.

We ask ourselves, who am I to be brilliant, gorgeous, talented, fabulous?

Actually, who are you NOT to be?

You are a child of God.

Your playing small does not serve the world.

There is nothing enlightened about shrinking so that other people won't feel insecure around you. We were born to make manifest the glory of God that is within us.

It is not just in some of us; it is in everyone.

And as we let our own Light shine, we unconsciously give other people permission to do the same.

As we are liberated from our own fear, our presence automatically liberates others.

This is also true of opening up as writers, and summoning the courage to write from the Soul. Courage is especially needed when supplying the one ingredient all stories must have: conflict.

Chapter 7

Story Conflict:
Holding the Tension of Opposites

Happy people have no history.
— Agatha Christie

MANY YEARS AGO, I was invited to talk to a class of nine-year-olds about writing. I asked them, "What if I wrote a story about two people who liked each other a lot, and never fought over anything — would that be an interesting story?"

"No!" they shouted. Even third graders knew, instinctively, that a story must have conflict. Without conflict, you have no story.

This is as true of comedy as it is of drama or tragedy. And in order to express conflict, you need characters. Notice that everything revolves around character in one way or another. Character is the axis of any story. Screenwriter Frank Pierson said in a Sundance Institute interview:

> The only thing that's important is the story, and the story arises from the conflict between the characters. And this you can only evolve by beginning with their needs and motives, bring them together, and they will create the story for you.

Sometimes when your characters are fully realized, they will take the reins, and all you have to do is hang on. It's a great ride when that happens. To have a great ride, however, requires conflict. And conflict requires a tension of opposites.

What do I mean by a *tension of opposites*, as shown in the chapter title above? C. G. Jung believed that every creative person is a synthesis of contradictory attitudes.

> A psychological truth is only true when the opposite is true.
> — C. G. Jung

Jung writes of opposing traits within one person, and how this tension creates movement. According to Jung, an archetype (mythic prototype) remains dormant until its opposite is aroused; then it is activated and the energy generated between them creates a *tertium quid*, a third thing — something new grows from that tension. This third thing is the life or story produced from the opposites. Without this tension of opposites or pull, there would be no life — and certainly there would be no true art.

Dramatic action is generated not only by tension between two characters but by tension within one central character. This is where the shadow lives, embracing our inherent contradictions between what we do and what we believe. The *shadow* is where the dark corners of the life live. Repressed, relegated to the unconscious. It is that part of the individual's unlived life that is sometimes either negatively or positively projected onto another person or group of people.

> Between the idea
> And the reality
> Between the motion
> And the act
> Falls the shadow
>   For Thine is the Kingdom.
> Between the conception
> And the creation
> Between the emotion
> And the response
> Falls the shadow.
>   Life is very long.
>   — T. S. Eliot, "The Hollow Men"

When Samuel Beckett writes a play, he sees it as a series of tensions. Two people might want the same object or territory or woman — and the tug of war begins. You might imagine a tug of war between the hero and antagonist. A good story — as life — is the tension between the opposites. Holding — or sustaining — this tension is what gives power to your story. You can observe the inner conflict projected outwards in a scene from Beckett's masterpiece, *Waiting for Godot*:

Estragon: We are all born mad. Some remain so...

Pozzo: Here! Here! Pity!

Estragon: It's revolting!

Vladimir: Quick! Give me your hand!

Estragon: I'm going. (Pause) I'm going.

Vladimir: Well I suppose in the end I'll get up by myself. (He tries, fails.) In the fullness of time.

Estragon: What's the matter with you?

Vladimir: Go to hell.

Estragon: Are you staying there?

Vladimir: Don't worry about me.

Estragon: Come on, Didi, don't be pig-headed!

> (He stretches out his hand which Vladimir makes haste to seize.)

Vladimir: Pull!

> (Estragon pulls, stumbles, falls. Long silence.)

Pozzo: Help!

Vladimir: We've arrived.

Pozzo: Who are you?

Vladimir: We are men.

> (Silence)

Samuel Beckett wrote this in 1954, and it is timeless, universal, for modern man remains caught in some existential void, busily going nowhere. Note the poetry of Beckett's despair, which lifts everything somehow. And every word returns us to the existential silence of not knowing.

An example from realism of dramatic tension would be Arthur Miller's *All My Sons* — as timely today as when it was written in 1947. The play's theme is the danger of corporate greed in America. It is the hidden lie of a past action that gives the play the necessary tension of opposites. A successful factory owner has made airplane parts on government contracts during World War II. One defective shipment of airplane parts was sent out anyway, causing a plane crash and the death of his son. The second son knows the truth and leaves home, returning years later to expose the lie to the third son who works with his father in the still-successful factory. At some point, the audience knows the secret before the other characters, and this also serves to create tension. We know *what* but not *when* the lie will be revealed or *how* it will affect the family.

An earlier example of dramatic tension is shown in *Oedipus Rex* by Sophocles, fifth-century BCE Greece. Here, the audience knows the secret before the main characters: that Oedipus has fulfilled the prophecy that he would kill his own father and marry his own mother. We know *what* will be revealed but not *when* or *how* it will affect the characters.

Note also that both of these examples are family dramas. It is no accident that the best of literature is a family drama of one kind or another. For a writer to work through his own father or mother complex — and yes, we all have them! — would fuel a life's work.

> That which is to give Light must endure burning.
> — Victor Frankl, *Man's Search for Meaning*

Other great family dramas which illustrate holding the tension or dramatic tension are *King Lear*, *Macbeth*, *Hamlet*, and most of the Greek tragedies. Eugene O'Neill's *Long Day's Journey into Night* — another family drama — holds the tension of the dark family secret until the last act. The secret is that though Eugene is dying, his father is too cheap to send him to a proper sanitarium. The most personal of the playwright's work and the best, O'Neill left instructions for the play not to be performed during his lifetime. The wound of the playwright's memory was still fresh.

Another way to fuel tension is to contrast your central characters. Create characters with different ages, social backgrounds, values or personalities, and you add more scope for conflict. Create complex characters which have opposing values within their own personality. Go against the stereotype. Do the unexpected. For instance, create a female serial killer who looks like an angel.

Another trick is to switch the gender of the character after completing the story. Hollywood did this with *Alien*, originally written for a male lead. What set the film apart and made it a colossal hit was that the action hero was converted into a heroine, played so well by Sigourney Weaver.

WRITE ABOUT WHAT BOTHERS YOU

The best writers learn to incorporate their own inner and outer conflicts into their stories. Playwright Tennessee Williams once commented that all artists are neurotic. The only difference between artists and other neurotics is that artists know how to channel their neurosis. Apart from whatever family ghosts you carry, there is the added tension arising from the risky business of earning a living from writing — the continuing uncertainties of the freelance world. Writers often swing from hope for success to fear of failure — a tension of opposites in itself. But tension can work — if you work it. To be an artist of any kind in a time in history that does not value the creative fields provides a continuing tension in relation to the art of survival. Still, you have the advantage of living your dream.

I remember once attending a party in New York City, after winning an award for playwriting. I was introduced to a doctor who said, "You know I always wanted to become a writer." I replied, "Then why didn't you?" He said that his father had been a doctor, and had expected him to become one, too. Despite the fact that this man earned a lot more than I did, I couldn't help but feel his loss.

> You pay a price for what you do, and you pay a price for what you don't do.
> — Louise Nevelson, sculptor

I suppose the plain truth is that you must choose which price to pay. Personally, I feel that those who do not follow their bliss pay the greater price.

However, know that though the grass may look greener on the other side, there are weeds there, too. Very few escape trials and tribulations. But these same trials build character. As Nietzsche said, "What doesn't kill you makes you stronger." It is the weeds in life that create the necessary tension to act and express. This tension is the fire that forges the vision, a fire which participates in a kind of alchemy of the soul — essential for life and art. It is the contrast and interaction between opposites which bring about change. Never forget that both light and dark are needed for transformation.

> All true things must change, and only that which changes remains true.
> — C. G. Jung

The challenge is to hold the tension and let it work within you in a creative, constructive manner. What is true for life is true for art. This inner tension aids in creating complex characters strong enough to hold the chaos.

> You must carry a chaos inside you to give birth to a dancing star.
> — Nietzsche

Oscar and Tony Award–winning director Mike Nichols (*Angels in America*) commented in the *Los Angeles Times*, "I've been lucky in that I can share my feelings and experiences on film. For me, they're grist. That really hurt, but, man, it's useful. Making movies heals the wounds."

The weekend invitation from the Baseball Hall of Fame in Cooperstown for an anniversary celebration of *Bull Durham* had been set up a year in advance, and actor Tim Robbins, a baseball fan and the film's star, had looked forward to bringing his whole family. Then, it was suddenly cancelled — due to Robbins' outspokenness against the war in Iraq. By coincidence, Robbins had been scheduled to speak in Washington D. C. at the National Press Club three days later, and had not yet prepared what to say.

Now he had a cause, and knew he would speak openly about this attempt to suppress free speech. Robbins warned that "there is a chill wind blowing in this nation... if you oppose this administration." Robbins further commented that "the cancellation turned out to be a gift because it galvanized me into writing." Here is a creative response to anger: self-expression.

> The creative principle must have opposition in order to exist.
> — Norman Mailer

Playwright Arthur Miller once told me a rather naughty — but true — story about Elia Kazan, who was directing the premiere production of *Death of a Salesman* on Broadway. Making sure to create the necessary friction between the two brothers, Kazan circulated false rumors about one actor to the other, causing the actors playing the brothers to soon detest one another. He got his effect, and the play made history.

Writers — as other artists — are often driven by something they may not understand. The trick is to channel the creative daemon before it turns demon or self-destructive. Vincent van Gogh, Nijinsky, Virginia Woolf, and Sylvia Plath are examples of artists being overtaken by their demons, at the end. Sometimes the greater the gift, the larger the demon.

> Where the light is brightest, the shadows are deepest.
> — Goethe

Novelist William Styron underwent a severe depression, and wrote a personal and courageous book about his struggles, *Darkness Visible: A Memoir of Madness*. He exorcised the dark demon. I last saw William Styron at a chamber music concert in New York, and a gentler and kindly man I have never met. Kindly men can sometimes harbor the darkest of demons.

> All suffering is bearable if it is seen as part of a story.
> — Isak Dinesen (*Out of Africa*)

Don't try to get rid of your demons. Channel them. Friends of Austrian poet Rainer Maria Rilke spoke to Sigmund Freud about Rilke who was undergoing a severe depression, and Freud agreed to analyze him. However, Rilke refused to see Freud, saying, "I know he would tame my demons, but I fear he might tamper with my angels."

Rilke endured his demon in order to protect his angel. In other words, creatively speaking, it's a package deal. Angels and demons abound in the psyche and are rich fodder for creativity. This is why many artists avoid psychotherapy, preferring to allow their creative work to provide the necessary release or channeling of those same inner contradictions. To protect the angels, as it were.

> Nothing resembles an angel so much as a demon, and vice versa.
> — Jean Dutourd

Inner voices are real. Why presume that something invisible is less real than what is physically perceived? Sometimes what is experienced within can be more real than a toaster or automobile. How does one prove Love, for instance? Or God? What are heaven and hell but aspects of ourselves? The inner conflict between darkness and light is the very heart of any good story. Who will win, good or evil? From Shakespeare to *Harry Potter* or Tolkien's *Lord of the Rings*, the battle between good and evil doesn't end — nor does its entertainment value.

Like Rilke, we must guard our inner angels — so necessary for creative work. They are such stuff as dreams are made on, the alchemical gold in your story, and what makes them truly yours. Yet do be kind to yourself along the way.

> A creative person has little power over his own life. He is not free. He is captive and driven by his daemon.
> — C. G. Jung

Life and work often overlap. Novelist Stephen King wrote a story, "Misery," about a successful writer hit by a car while walking on the highway — and later this actually happened to him. Other times the life event will occur first and inspire a story.

During a life crisis of my own, I decided, after years of conflict, to leave a nineteen-year marriage. Then, after the divorce, I sat down and wrote my angriest play, *The Myth of Annie Beckman*. It is a fictional story about a woman pushed over the edge — only the *feelings* are real. The play ends in unspeakable tragedy. Fortunately, my life didn't. Both acting and writing have been, for me, the greatest of therapies. I have committed suicide in four different plays when I acted as Juliet in *Romeo and Juliet*, Anna Karenina in *Anna K*, Cassandra in *The Trojan Women*, and one of the thirteen characters I played in Edgar Lee Master's *Spoon River Anthology*. Now I had written of an attempted suicide in one play of my own.

When *The Myth of Annie Beckman* was performed at The Actor's Studio in New York, there was an open discussion led afterwards by director Arthur Penn (*Bonnie and Clyde*). Usually, a moderator is expected to be neutral, but not this time. Arthur Penn stood up and denounced my play as not believable. "No woman would say or do such things. Not possible." Suddenly a wave of angry cries rose up from the audience: women protesting that they can and they do, citing specific examples from their own lives and those of their friends. The play tells of a modern day Medea — pushed over the edge by an unfaithful yet demanding husband — who kills her young, hyperactive son, then tries to kill herself — only she lives.

I feel there is an angel in me whom I am constantly shocking.
— Jean Cocteau

The point here is that it's better to write of such horrors than to remain silent and do them. (This is incidentally the best of arguments not to cut funding for the arts in public schools. It cannot be overstated how utterly crucial it is for young people to learn to appropriately channel their passions.)

It might be useful to share the seed origin of the fictional character of Annie Beckman. I had just completed a term of teaching at The New School University, flown to the premiere of my new play, *Calamity Jane,* and was now flying to India with my young son. Though not hyperactive, he was an extremely bright and active elementary school child. We stopped in Geneva for half a day to break the arduous journey. I had had precious little sleep in the last weeks due to play re-writes and teaching. My son could not sleep, and wanted to talk and talk and talk. At one moment, I over-reacted, raised my hand, and *almost* struck him — something I had never done before. What shocked me was that I realized that from sleep deprivation and nerves, I *felt* I was capable of doing anything in order to sleep. Later, I drew upon this feeling to create Annie Beckman — a woman who, in final desperation, tosses her four-year-old son out of her apartment window in New York City — then jumps herself. A writer feels the feeling then pushes it to an extreme. It is the extreme in any story which gives it power.

> We are two things at once. At best, we are close to noble, and at worst, we are comic and sometimes God-awful.
> — Norman Mailer

Mailer saw my play performed in New York City, introduced himself, and said how moved he was. I asked if he would send me his response in a letter as I was soon to apply for a writing grant. Graciously, he later sent me the following letter, which luckily, I recently discovered in my papers:

> The play had a rare and substantial power. I say substantial because at certain instants of denouement, the hair rose on my neck, which is not a sensation I am accustomed to, in fact, I don't remember it occurring before. Though a young play-wright, she is in possession of a most powerful talent, because *The Myth of Annie Beckman* puts us in the presence of genuine tragedy, and nothing is more rare in my opinion than to be able to conceive of such a work in our modern theatre.

As my Texas mother says, "It never hurts to ask." Though I had never before met Norman Mailer, I had acted with two of his ex-wives, and knew that this brilliant novelist was certainly possessed of his own private demon. Here was a man who understood both the dangers and the salvation of the creative process.

> Every creative person is a synthesis of contradictory attitudes: a human being with a personal life and on the other, an imper-sonal creative process.
> — C. G. Jung

Perhaps the best antidote to the pitfalls of the creative life is not to divide one's art from one's living. All too often, artists pour the best of themselves into their work, and the worst into their life and relationships.

Is conflict needed for the creative process? Absolutely. Unfortunately though, the tensions and conflicts of the creative process all too often spill over into the personal life. Artists are often subject to moods during the creative process. I always considered myself an actor who leaves my character at the theatre. However, this is true only after finding the character. There is a point during rehearsals — usually about the third week — where I sometimes cannot distinguish between myself and the role. My family has commented that during this week, I am not fun to be around. It must be confusing as well, for your child to suddenly hear you speaking in a strange voice and walking differently. However, once I have the character, and the play opens — then I can settle into the run of the play, leaving the character behind in the dressing room along with the costume.

Even as a writer, I notice sometimes that I am overtaken by those I write about. This occurred when I was hired to write a biographical feature film of Edgar Allan Poe. Mallarmé, poet and translator of Poe into French, referred to the tortured American writer as "the dark angel." So I called the screenplay *Poe: The Dark Angel.* During this time, my thoughts and moods were darker than usual, my sleep troubled. I was more than relieved when I finished this screenplay!

> I disagree with the notion that everything in a work of art must be easily comprehended and pleasantly obvious at whatever price. An author must have the right to keep certain things concealed in the mystical and obscure. Ivan Karamazov lives his ideas. They are made concrete through his destiny. Person and idea are fused together.
> — Dostoyevsky

There is also a similar tension or war within the hero himself. An internal war is fought in each of us — and it is usually underground. Man is an immortal essence trapped in a mortal body, and this is the field where the opposites meet.

Spending time in art museums can fuel your writing and strengthen the emotions required to fill your characters. Color, for instance, expresses *feeling* — especially in modern art. The grueling self-portraits of contemporary painter Lucien Freud are well worth viewing to express the inner tension of opposites. The viewer can see the internal battle within the artist expressed with a ruthless honesty on canvas. Imagine the inner chaos that produced van Gogh's black crows and trembling sunflowers. How to portray the yellow in van Gogh's sunflowers or the despair of his black crows? What is their equivalent in words?

The swing or oscillation between transcendence and sinking into the quagmire is the polarity of life and art.

> The world into which we are born is brutal and cruel, and at the same time, of divine beauty.
> — C. G. Jung

Imagine the turmoil which gave us Eugene O'Neill's masterpiece about his own dysfunctional family, *Long Day's Journey into Night*, or T. S. Eliot's *The Wasteland* which in one poem defined for a generation the agonies of war. Eliot wrote this while dealing with his own private war: loving and living with a mad wife in "rats alley."

Writing about whatever horrors might arise in your mind gives voice to emotions that will mirror those of others, providing insight into the lives of your readers or audience. To find the universal (collective), seek the specific (personal).

Holding the tension of opposites, going to and from the edge of these extremes will create dramatic action. If this is to work, it is crucial to allow sufficient space and rhythm for your reader or audience's not knowing. That is, don't reveal too much of either plot or character in the telling of your story. It is usually best to dole out exposition — or information about your main characters — a little at a time. Not only in mysteries, but in all genres, allow the lies to be stripped away bit by bit, revealing the truth of the character and what he or she has done or is.

Two failings of new writers are:

1) Revealing too much too soon
2) Having their characters be too perfect.

I've observed with students and workshop participants an unfortunate tendency to create main characters without flaws. *Wabi-sabi*, the Japanese law of aesthetics, means a beauty of things imperfect, impermanent, and incomplete. A master potter in Japan, as a final step in producing a classic pot, purposely creates a flaw in what otherwise would seem perfection. The perfection is in the flaw. Shakespeare knew this well. His most famous protagonists had them:

Macbeth (both Mr. and Mrs.) — ruthless ambition
Hamlet — inability to act
Othello — jealousy
Falstaff — his love for Prince Hal

The tragic flaw is the character's Achilles heel through which his downfall occurs. The popular dramatic series *The Sopranos* is a good example of flawed characters, not revealing too much too soon, and stripping away the lies. Virginia Heffernan interviews the show's creator, writer, and producer, David Chase, for the *New York Times*.

The main character, Tony Soprano, is urging Christopher to avenge his father's killing. Tony wants Christopher to be his successor and wants to toughen him up.

Christopher is becoming sentimental about his lost father, and recalls that his father was carrying a crib for him home when he was shot down. And Tony says, "It was a stack of TV trays, actually. But it could have been a crib." Here is David Chase's response:

I wrote that. Everything that everybody says is untrue. Complete falsehoods, self-justifications, rationalizations, lies, fantasies, and miscommunication... These people are lying to themselves and to each other all the time... I would imagine that the more time you spend talking to another person, the more you lie to them. So if you spend a lot of time with your relations, you're probably lying a lot to them.

Drama is the search for wholeness that embraces contradictions. Dramatic action might be seen as the process and tensions whereby the lies are stripped away. Imagine a wall which stands between two of your characters. The wall is the lies surrounding their lives, and scene by scene, the lies will be stripped away until your main character stands naked, stripped of all the lies.

Art is a lie which allows us to approach the truth.
— Picasso

EXERCISE

Draw a line down a page, your wall separating the character's contradictions from his actions or truth. List the contradictions. Then write a short scene where little by little the lies are stripped away, exposing the character. Have one character expose the other character, making him or her vulnerable. Push it to an extreme, as to the effect it has on the exposed character.

A good illustration of not revealing too much or having the main characters not be overly perfect (without flaw) is Horton Foote's screenplay *Tender Mercies* which won Oscars for both Foote and actor Robert Duvall. In the beginning Duvall's character is seen as a penniless drunk. Only later do we discover that he was once a famous songwriter and singer. His flaw was evident from the opening scene. The story shows his journey towards sobriety and the recovery of his dream and purpose to live.

Conflict is embedded in us from the beginning. Life is a battle. First we fight each other, then ourselves or the other way round.

> We are an animal, which, when cornered, becomes eloquent.
> — Graham Greene

Sometimes becoming a mirror for the collective can be a bit risky. The theme of my play *Somewhere-in-Between* is how to remain sane in a world gone mad. One evening in New York after a performance, a rather excited woman asked to meet the playwright, and was convinced that I understood her problems better than anyone. She had completely identified with the character of the schizophrenic, and because of this, trusted me and sought help. She attached herself to me like a barnacle. I left the theatre. She followed. After three blocks of listening to a rather frantic confessional monologue, I had to tell her that I was not a psychiatrist, and perhaps she should seek professional help. Such is the power of mirroring!

The novels of Dostoyevsky, for instance, give the impression of a battle over unsolved problems. His own obsession with gambling fills *Crime and Punishment* as his search for spiritual values infuses both *The Brothers Karamazov* and *The Idiot*. Write about those issues you wish to solve, those you feel passionate about.

THE BEST STORIES HAVE THREE LEVELS OF CONFLICT:

External Conflict — war, earthquake, corporate takeover, labor strike, etc.

Interpersonal Conflict — between main characters

Inner Conflict — within your main character

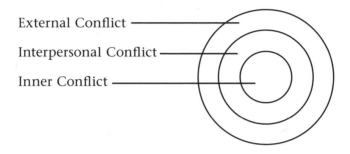

External Conflict

Interpersonal Conflict

Inner Conflict

1. *Chinatown* (1974) written by Oscar-winning screenwriter Robert Towne is a good example. Jack Nicholson (Oscar winner) plays a detective caught in a corporate scandal.

External conflict: Water monopoly scandal in Los Angeles

Interpersonal conflict: Nicholson-Faye Dunaway; Nicholson-John Huston; Nicholson-police

Inner conflict: Nicholson and his Chinatown past, his ghost

2. *Casablanca* (1942) written by Oscar winners Julius and Philip Epstein and Howard Koch. And Humphrey Bogart plays Rick.

External conflict: World War II

Interpersonal conflict: Bogart-Ingrid Bergman, Bogart-Claude Rains, Bogart-Nazis.

Inner conflict: Bogart's fear of loving and trusting her again, and also the tension or pull between wanting to run off with her and doing the right thing: a greater purpose.

3. *The Quiet American* (2002) written by Christopher Hampton and Robert Schenkkan, adapted from Graham Greene's novel. Michael Caine plays Thomas Fowler and Brendan Fraser plays Alden Pyle.

External conflict: the French and American involvement in Viet Nam, 1952.

Interpersonal conflict: the two men in love with the same woman, as well as the conflict of interest between their respective countries.

Inner conflict: betraying a friendship due to romantic and political interests.

The writer who aims high will attempt to unite the contradictory opposites, and provide a true catharsis for his reader or audience — as in the three examples above. This need not mean a happy ending, only an emotionally satisfying one possessing some resolution, and usually a moral revelation of some kind.

Each of us seeks a way to unite the opposites, returning to the One. This is the motivating force of all action and behavior, either knowingly or unknowingly. Lovers are drawn to one another in order to make two into one. The superb American novelist, Willa Cather, once remarked that we spend half of our lives reaching out to another human being, and the other half of our lives, pulling away. Here is a tension of opposites that creates story.

The only difference between vision and hallucination is the capacity to give form and meaning. This distinguishes the artist from the insane. Artists, struggling with their inner demon, are often said to possess a touch of madness. This touch of madness is creativity, and therefore all the more precious in an increasingly literal and conformist society. Someone once remarked that the poet William Blake was cracked. Hearing this, the English poetess, Edith Sitwell, quipped, "Yes, that is where the Light shines through."

> There is a price on everything in life. Anything of great value carries its shadow zone with it. There is no escaping it. Every positive value has its price in negative terms and you never see anything great which is not, at the same time, horrible in some respect. The genius of Einstein leads to Hiroshima.
> — Pablo Picasso

We strive for order in our lives, for constancy, for something to believe in. But human experience is far from perfect, even contradictory. Allow the contradictions. Follow them, expose them, and you will find your story.

Chapter 8

Awakening the Inner Eye:

From Dream to Disney

I see visions which I could not see with my ordinary eye.
— Maxine Hong Kingston (*Woman Warrior*)

IT IS MY feeling that some stories already exist in the ether, and my job is simply to bring them down to the gross level. The best times are when I seem to disappear altogether and the story writes itself. It passes through me, but is not really mine — a kind of visitation, if you will.

This process of listening to the unconscious is greatly aided by listening and recording your dreams, which inevitably speak the language of the unconscious, and can serve as guide. William Blake might refer to this as "the crooked way being the right way."

Sometimes story ideas may come through dreams at night. This is why I suggest keeping a journal or notebook near your bed, in order to catch the dream — which might otherwise prove elusive.

One night I dreamt of an *angel* returned to earth because he was not yet ready for heaven. Denied his wings because he was still too attached to earthly pleasures, he was asked to undergo a trial on earth, to earn his wings. I recorded the dream in my journal, then thought no more about it. About ten days later, my agent had a call from megastar Dolly Parton's company. Dolly had been scouting for a good Christmas story for television, and after two years, had not found one she liked. Because of the success of my film, *The Christmas Wife*, they thought I might come up with something. Immediately, I thought of the angel dream. I switched genders from male to female angel, and while driving to Los Angeles, developed the story, set it two weeks before Christmas, and called it *Unlikely Angel*.

Now, please understand that I do not read magazines or *Variety*, or other books which talk about what stars like. I was simply guided by my intuition — a faculty I have come to trust much more than the rational brain. So I was not aware that Dolly Parton is simply mad about angels. I walked into her Hollywood home and saw angel sculptures in the garden, a tapestry of angels on the wall, and little angel ornaments placed here and there on several tables. Bingo! I was home free. This story would sell. And it did, to Disney Studios. Hence, the title of this chapter: *From Dream to Disney*. The moral: pay attention to your dreams!

Of course, many writers have the experience of receiving stories or insights through their dreams or from somewhere beyond. Stephen King, master horror storyteller, sees stories as relics of a pre-existing world. The writer must dig them up like fossils. He calls it thinking above the curve. Whatever you choose to call it, creative writing is not a logical process. No neat formula can replace the golden story seeds stored in your unconscious.

How to develop the intuitive skills necessary to access images? We are taught many things in school, but all too often, this is linear learning, textbook learning. I can remember sitting in classrooms as a child staring aimlessly out of the window at passing clouds. The teacher's verdict was I was wasting my time, yet who is to say that daydreaming is less valuable than memorizing a list of facts. Thomas Edison was a daydreamer. He pondered, "What if there could be light in a small bulb powered by electricity?"

For the mind to be creative, there must be stillness.
— J. Krishnamurti

Non-creatives often forget how important unscheduled time is for a writer. This seems particularly true of those who hire writers. In the early Hollywood days when writers were kept at the motion picture studios in offices, they were supposed to be writing all day long. In fact, there is a story of Louis B. Mayer — then head of MGM — routinely walking by the doors of the writers' wing, his ear to the door to see if the typewriters were clicking!

Sometimes the best writing occurs when the writer is not physically writing. Once I was stumped while writing an original comedy feature for Universal Studios. I knew the *what*, but not the *how*. So I did what has become my process: stopped writing. I went swimming instead. About the eleventh lap with my mind utterly blank, the solution appeared. My conscious mind could not find the solution to the story, so I let go, and allowed my mind to drift and dream.

> Significant problems cannot be solved at the same level of the thinking which created them.
> — Albert Einstein

The solution appeared as a gift from the invisibles, allowing me to go back to the desk and make my deadline for the Studio.

> Stay at your table and listen. Don't even listen, just wait, be completely quiet and alone. The world will offer itself to you to be unmasked.
> — Franz Kafka

A famous mathematician from India called Ramanujan, was asked later when he was at Oxford University, how he came up with such remarkable mathematical discoveries when he was only a humble clerk from Madras. He replied that at night when he was asleep, the Goddess Devi would come and whisper in his ear, telling him the solutions.

> As soon as the least of us stands still that's the moment something extraordinary is seen to be going on in the world.
> — Eudora Welty

A writer sometimes needs to do nothing. He may seem to be doing nothing yet in fact he is tuning out the outer world in order to allow the inner intuitive mind, to drift and dream. For those that remember, before television and computer games, there was cloud-gazing — a spiritual, introspective pursuit with no goal whatsoever.

> I saw myself when I shut my eyes: space, space, where I am and am not.
> — Octavio Paz, Nobel poet

Today, in a society which values quick results, kids are scheduled to death. Age five or younger: gymnastics, dance, and play dates. What became of solitary play, block building, tree climbs, and general, aimless wanderings? These were the blessings of my Texas childhood. The best parts of my childhood were the leisurely unscheduled hours and hours, I — an only child — was let be. This allowed imagination to develop. To these rich empty spaces of childhood, I attribute my own beginnings as a storyteller. Imagination cannot be assumed. It must be fostered, valued.

> Imagination is more important than knowledge.
> — Albert Einstein

When my son was age two to four years, we lived in a small village in south India. What toys he had were made from coconut palm leaf and other natural substances. We made up stories every night before bedtime. I did manage to obtain paper and crayons at a nearby town. My proudest moment was when I asked my son to draw Love, and, without the slightest hesitation, he drew wide blue circles on the paper. He drew as he experienced, or felt. Now, years later, I want my students and clients to do the same (with the necessary craft to support their vision).

> To write is to create a space in which things can happen. To live one's life, the same.
> — Michael Adam (*Man Is a Little World*)

As children at play, we are organically aware of empty space. Whether a floor or sandbox or lawn, the first thing a child does is clear the space for play. Out of this empty space, the subject of play — whatever it may be — will spontaneously arise from within the child's imagination. *And the child will look upon his creation and know that it is good.* Whether a tall building or jungle, dog or giant, the child will neither fear the empty space from which its creation will arise nor compare his creation with that of yesterday. All that exists for him is now and the empty space waiting to be filled.

> Every child is an artist. The problem is how to remain an artist once he grows up.
> — Pablo Picasso

Of course, this is so only for the very young pre-school child, for quite soon this wonderfully imaginative child will be conditioned away from freely inhabiting this empty space. He will be *educated* into right and wrong, better and worse, and all manner of comparatives which inhibit the spontaneity of creating space. He will become conscious of the right way to do things. "The sky must be blue; the grass only green." Thus creation becomes less and less necessary, even extinct. And how to begin to express my concern to live in a society where creativity is not only undervalued, but all but extinct? Remember, a culture defines itself by what it values.

Years ago, during my playwriting days in New York, I was invited by the Dramatist Guild (playwrights guild) to lead playwriting workshops in public schools in New York City, as part of the Young Playwrights Festival annual competition. In a high school in the South Bronx, I noticed policemen walking the halls with guns. There was trouble in the school and the police had been called in to daily patrol the halls. I later learned that the powers that be had cut both the athletic funds as well as the art funds from the school. This meant youth with raging hormones had no outlet either physically (team sports) or emotionally (arts). Yet somehow no one had connected these funding cuts with the recent outburst of violence!

Beware the effects of a fragmented society. Creativity is vital for a balanced society, that is, in the schools, not because everyone might become an artist one day, but because the arts develop the heart — not only the rational mind. I don't know about anyone else, but I would hope that whoever holds the power to push the red button for nuclear war had a balanced education of both heart and mind. I would hope my President had read Shakespeare, listened to Mozart, and, in a moment of stillness, pondered Monet's paintings of Givenchy water lilies.

> Demonism and creativity are psychologically very close to each other. Nothing in the human psyche is more destructive than unrealized, unconscious creative impulses... When it is a question of a mass psychosis, nothing but new, creative conceptions, brought up from the depth, can stop the development toward a catastrophe.
> — C. G. Jung

Like dreams, creativity arises from the unconscious. We have to create an empty space in our conscious minds for the unconscious to emerge with its gifts. Our conditioning prods us to rush in with interpretative meaning, learned meanings, which may serve only to flatten the true value of what arises naturally from within. Mental understanding won't necessarily change us. To be transformed requires something more than rational thinking or sentimentalism. The conditioned way of mental knowing often strengthens the ego at the expense of soul. In fact, mere mental understanding may be overrated today. Marc Chagall said of his paintings that he didn't understand them at all. "They are only pictorial arrangements of images that obsess me."

In the best art, form is the outcome of feeling, not thinking. Thinking — though a valuable tool — is only handmaiden to a deeper process.

> It is the inexplicable presence of the thing not named... the emotional aura that gives high quality to the novel or to drama, as well as to poetry itself.
> — Willa Cather

It was the Christmas holidays and I simply did not feel like writing this book. After an hour of forcing or "pushing the river," I sensibly decided to let it go for a while. Later that day, I was on my way to Los Angeles to meet friends for a play and dinner. In the car, suddenly ideas of what to add to this book kept popping up. I jotted the three ideas down while driving, and the next day added them. I had let go of the book for the day, but my unconscious had not! There are indeed invisible helpers at work when you least expect them!

> I can't understand these chaps who go around American univer-
> sities explaining how they write. It's like going round explaining
> how you sleep with your wife.
> — Philip Larkin

I must confess that even after writing professionally for twenty-five years, my writing approach or process may unexpectedly change. From my own professional experience, I have often found that the process must adapt to the story at hand. For instance, generally speaking, I first write an outline and then write the story, play, or script in the order it will be read, chronologically. That is, beginning on page one, and plowing through without edits or revisions, to the end. This I had come to understand was my process. Imagine my surprise — writing this book — when ideas would appear that belonged in a much later chapter. Eventually, I gave in and followed what was to me a new approach or process. For instance, I might write a few pages of the final chapter before returning to Chapter 6. Also, against my earlier habit of plowing through to the end without re-crafting, now, with this book, I rewrite daily. (I assume, Dear Reader, you will find no disadvantage here, as when the book is done, you may read the chapters in the order published.)

If you are writing a mystery and wish to begin with the discovery of who did it, do so and work backwards. All roads lead to Rome. Discover your own process by listening to those inner voices. Allow yourself the freedom to alter your own writing process, project to project.

> In the dry woods a dragon is singing. I do not know what kind
> of composition the dragon's song is, but all those who hear it
> lose themselves.
> — Hsiang-yen

Sometimes a sensation type will find his writing path through the senses, feeling what he writes in his own body, not only the emotions. One novelist turned the literary world upside down with a novel called *Lady Chatterley's Lover.* Readers were so shocked to be asked to feel with their bodies that the book was banned.

> My God, I can only say I touch, I feel the unknown... I have found the other world.
> — D. H. Lawrence, *A New Heaven and a New Earth*

SENSORY EXERCISE

Sit quietly for a moment and simply feel your body. Now imagine you are naked lying in the sun. Stay with the feeling, feel it specifically all over your body. Now allow your mind to free associate. You might think of someone you love or when you were a small child. Go with the images. Now pick up your pen and describe a character undergoing some trial or peak experience where the feelings are raw and visceral.

MEMORY EXERCISE

Choose a family photo of one of your parents, grandparents, or a lover. Sit quietly in front of the photograph, allowing your mind to drift into memories of things past. Close your eyes. Try to remember how this person smelled. Recall their touch. Then, whether the experience is positive or negative, describe it in words from a *feeling* perspective. Find an image (bird, animal, or object) to represent your character and how he or she would move and behave.

Sometimes, in my workshops, a writer will find his story simply by doing these exercises.

> The artist's whole business is to make something out of nothing.
> — Paul Valery

IMAGES REMEMBERED AND IMAGINED

> All things create themselves from their own innermost
> reflection and none can tell how they came to do so.
>   — Chuang Tzu

Even before there are stories, there are images. Each life is formed
by its unique image, an image that is the essence of that life and
that calls it to destiny. To discover the image of our theme or main
character, we must enter the invisible world and allow it to carry
us. Intuitive images occur, we cannot make them. All we can do is
get out of the way, thereby inviting them to come through.

> The history of man is the history of images.
>   — Wallace Stevens

A wonderful way to find story ideas is in books of photographs,
or gallery and museum exhibits of photographs. You might find a
character image or story idea. The coffee table books of *Life* magazine are particularly good examples. Or you might try a book of
Dorothea Lange's haunting images of the Depression in America.
John Steinbeck was hired to write copy for Depression photographs
in California of the migrant fruit workers. This inspired him to
write the *The Grapes of Wrath*. The film adaptation then drew on
these photographs as a set up for several shots in the movie.

> A picture is worth a thousand words.
>   — Old Chinese saying

Andy Warhol, who began as a graphic designer for advertising,
focused his art on American icons or images that have become
signposts for an era. Images as Marilyn Monroe, John F. Kennedy,
and Campbell Soup cans all bespeak America. What makes them
work as art is that the audience identifies with these images.

Similarly, the emotional power of a story is often felt through
visual images. Images are the natural language of the unconscious.
Psyche is revealed through images as in dreams. And the darkest
image may prove the most valuable. Consider Kafka's cockroach in
Metamorphosis or Dante's images of hell in his *Inferno*.

The intolerable image is the transformational image.
— Wallace Stevens

The soul of writing comes through the image — what Keats called "soul-making." Images are the language of the soul. They integrate mind, body, and soul and thereby serve a healing function. When Shakespeare writes, "Out, out brief candle", he is using the language of metaphor or imaging. He does not say, "Out, out brief life." The metaphorical or symbolic image lifts the reader above the gross level to a realm of poetry where image and soul reign. This is where transformation occurs.

The poet is the priest of the invisible.
— Wallace Stevens

Real doing comes from stillness — not endless busyness or even reading. Perhaps now is a good time to set this book down for a time, after reading and doing the following exercise.

CHANNELING EXERCISE

Take a moment, visualize clearly what you want to write, then sink deep into yourself before the inevitable action of writing. Close your eyes, feel what is going on within. Then without undue thought, pick up your pen and write whatever wants to come. On channeling: Let it come through you, not from you. Dare to be surprised!

Some version of the above exercise might become a simple, daily ritual. Some writers might light a candle or do a brief meditation or visualization, visualizing the story before sitting down to write it. Or you can play music that makes you soar. In this way, a dimension of the sacred is added — an invitation extended to those invisible helpers mentioned earlier.

You don't just get a story. You just have to wait for it to come to you. I've never written a story in my life. The story has come to me and demanded to be written.
— Somerset Maugham

Writing, like life, is a process. You can't rush it. Story — like any other important relationship — needs time. As Shakespeare rightly said, "Ripeness is all." Furthermore, I have come to believe that more often than not, the story chooses its own time. Here's one example. Many years ago, long before I began to write professionally, I was in Ireland on my honeymoon. I had been rather psychic since childhood and, fortunately, married a man who took such things seriously. We were at a monastic ruin near Athloane when I began to see a violent story unfold as in a waking dream. Years passed, and this Irish story kept nipping at my heels like some persistent puppy. I call this the story idea that won't let you go. These are usually the stories that one day must be written. However, sometimes the story will choose its own time, as well.

Flash forward twenty-three years after the initial vision which occurred during my Irish honeymoon. I am in a library browsing in the history section. Often, I walk by, touching the various books as I read the titles, not looking for anything in particular. This way I invite my intuitive faculty to choose. Accidentally, a book fell from the shelf. It opened to a particular section, so naturally I picked it up and read it. Imagine my surprise when it described a Viking invasion at the very same monastery near Athloane, Ireland! It also gave two specifics which I had included in my story notes. What I saw so many years ago in a waking vision at that monastic ruin in Ireland actually happened — back in the ninth century.

> There are more things in heaven and earth, Horatio, than are dreamt of in your philosophy.
> — William Shakespeare, *Hamlet*

This makes me think of Plato's over-soul idea: that all Knowledge exists floating above us, and that it is possible to tap into it. At least, this was the experience of writing *Second Chance*, a reincarnation love story set in ninth-century Ireland. Though the seed of this story was planted during my years as an actress, then a playwright, it was only when I began writing films in Hollywood that the Irish story summoned. It happened like this.

A newcomer to Hollywood, I had just signed a contract to write a Hallmark Hall of Fame television movie (*Summertime*) and had a deadline to meet. So I sat down intending to write the two-hour teleplay, but instead the old Irish story surfaced after twenty-three years, commanding my attention, holding me captive. Within ten days, the original feature screenplay, *Second Chance*, was written. It was as if I did little more than type, for the story seem to pour through me from somewhere else, channeled. It poured through effortlessly, written as if *remembered*. Forces are at work here and although they may defy rational explanations, they may be deeply *experienced* — if not always understood.

> Good fiction is partly a bringing of the news from one world to another.
> — Raymond Carver

Second Chance took a long time from vision to page, and I suspect — though it has been optioned twice — it will be produced on the screen at exactly the right time. Its own time, not mine.

> The artist must attune himself to that which wants to reveal itself and permit the process to happen through him.
> — Martin Heidegger

Of course, this holds true for all the arts.

> The painting has a life of its own. I try to let it come through.
> — Jackson Pollack

Pollack worked from his feeling function, and the viewer cannot help but have a feeling response when standing before his explosive paintings.

The only difference between vision and hallucination is the capacity to give form and meaning. This distinguishes the artist from the insane. Artists are often said to possess a touch of madness. This touch of madness is creativity, and therefore all the more precious in an increasingly conformist society.

> God robbed poets of their minds that they might be made expressions of His own.
> — Theodore Roethke, poet

How to invite your story through visualization? The moments remembered in a great novel or film are usually visual moments, unspoken moments. Virtual reality without technology. Memory is one of the primal sources for creative images. How we remember is how we give meaning to a life lived.

> A novel is never anything but a philosophy expressed in images.
> — Albert Camus

When the inner work goes well, unobstructed by outer events or inner attitudes, synchronicities abound. *Synchronicity*, according to C. G. Jung, is a meaningful coincidence. Jung drew from philosopher Arthur Schopenhauer, who had postulated a link between simultaneous events which were causally unconnected. Jung's idea is that synchronicity is based on a universal order of meaning.

SYNCHRONICITY: THE HUMMINGBIRD STORY

Psychologist Veronica Goodchild, in a talk at the *Portals to the Sacred* seminars at Pacifica Graduate Institute in Santa Barbara, CA, cites her most difficult case which she refers to as *The Hummingbird*.

Unspeakable acts of abuse and terror were experienced in the patient's childhood, leaving a feeling of despair in both therapist and patient. How could healing take place after such horror? Even the therapist had begun to lose faith confronted with this patient exemplifying the split between light and dark faces of God. Only in Love could there be hope for change. Then a miracle occurred. A hummingbird appeared just outside the window above the head of the patient. Dr. Goodchild was moved and called her patient's attention to the hummingbird. Suddenly the patient broke into smiles and revealed that her non-American name means hummingbird. She had been considering changing back to this original name. At this moment, the whole office atmosphere changed as her meaning and destiny had appeared.

> All things create themselves.
> — Lao Tzu

Here a synchronicity took place — invisible helpers — which provoked the necessary healing for both patient and therapist.

In art, we find ourselves experiencing reality on more than one plane. The creative act is thus an act of liberation — the defeat of habit by originality. The creative process does not travel in straight lines. It thrives in the undefined spaces in between.

Sometimes, an image without a story may come to you through your dreams. It is important to keep your right-brain muscles well-toned. Here is a personal example of how to work with images in your dreams. A while back, I was having a series of dreams involving owls. The owl dreams — as I refer to them — moved and stayed with me for days and days, felt as a kind of unseen presence. Though I cannot say what the full meaning of this dream is, I do know that it remains with me as a living presence or guide. Here is one of the owl dreams:

> I am walking down a wide, unpaved road. I see a great white owl flying straight at me then swooping over my head to the left. I am not afraid. Then I notice an identical three foot tall, white owl with brown specks standing next to me on my right, gently staring at me. We gaze at each other for some time. Then the owl flies off with silent wings. Next I see three large buffalo, but am uncertain whether they are real or spirit buffalo as an aura surrounds their bodies. Ahead, I see a large oak tree with many branches but no leaves. Thirteen large ravens are perched on the branches. They are black and white, very still, and seem to herald some message. Upon awakening, there is the distinct feeling of this being more than a dream — more a visitation.

The following morning after the dream, it was reported in the news that a white buffalo, considered sacred to Native Americans, had been born. However, the strongest presence in the dream was the large white owl standing to my right, offering a kind of energy transmission by gently staring at me. This owl became the focused dream image. I had characteristically *thought* about all manner of owl associations, both personal and collective, and written these down, gathering knowledge, from being considered a symbol of the goddess Minerva, and various Native American symbols. Then I took a quiet moment and simply sat with the image of the owl — without trying to analyze anything. From this arose a powerful *felt sense* of the owl. I sank deeper into myself, and felt the owl or owl-ness surround my entire body. I disappeared into the great owl yet retained my own form. Its spirit lay as a protective cover and poured into me. I became still, mind was no more, and the feeling of a mighty blessing overcame me. Energy as circles of light swirled in my heart chakra while a gentle tingling filled the whole body. Tears of gratitude and awe filled my eyes. What exactly had transpired here?

Jungian analyst James Hillman says the aim of the dream is to redress a supposed lost balance. As a conditioned child who had lost its empty space, I had been educated away from a deeper soul balance. Owl came to redress this balance, to center me. But the experience came not from mental activity, but by letting go of the gathering busy mind, sinking down into the body, and allowing the dream image to work on me. In other words, the owl image had moved from concept to experience. Experience — though spiritual in nature — was grounded in body awareness. As a child filling empty space, I had invited the dream image of owl to inhabit me. And it was good.

Owl is also seen as a messenger of death. The day before the dream, a known singer and former friend had committed suicide by jumping out of a New York window because her career had slumped. I heard the news on National Public Radio driving home from Los Angeles. We were the same age, and though I had not seen her for some years, I understood all too well the despair of the precarious twists and turns of a freelance career in the arts today.

Another attribute of owl is waiting. Waiting is also a way of creating space and time where the real can occur. Sometimes at transitional times, waiting is the wisest course — though the most difficult. Jungian James Hillman says, "To look at animals from an underworld perspective means to regard them as carriers of soul... there to help us see in the dark."

I petition owl to remain on my rational shoulder and guide me through the underworld to the light of whatever tomorrow may bring. In ways like these, ancient myths come alive and live through us today.

Silent wings, sharp beak
Seer and hunter of the night.
Owl wisdom.

Let intuition guide. Story is ultimately a metaphor or symbolic image of what you are trying to say. It is through metaphor that the process of life and art can be seen as in a mirror. Look for metaphors in both waking and dream states. Awaken that part of the mind that generates images. Dare to explore the unknown regions of the psyche, for therein lies creative gold.

Metaphor is the language of the soul. Well-chosen images can help us integrate mind and feeling which in today's culture has been split asunder. There is no greater path than the path to wholeness. Write with your senses, feelings, and invisible wonderings. Write stories that serve soul.

The visionary is the only true realist.
— Fellini

Chapter 9
The Voice of the Story

How do I know about the world? By what is within me.
— Lao Tzu

*T*HE HEALING FUNCTION of good writing for both the writer and his audience depends on making it one's own from within. The challenge always is to find your own voice which conveys the power of a particular story. How you feel about what you are writing, your individual values, expresses your relationship to the material. In other words, this makes possible your POV or point of view. Here, authenticity is vital.

Listen. Make a way for yourself inside yourself.
— Rumi

THE WRITER'S VOICE

Writers usually have a point of view about whatever they are writing about. They have the opportunity to represent history using a specific story, with their own point of view providing a distinctive view of the world. Aristophanes in fifth-century BCE Greece wrote an anti-war play called *Lysistrata* in which the Athenian women banded together and refused sexual favors to their husbands until they agreed to stop fighting. Funny, yes, but the point is clearly made.

What would happen if one woman told the truth about her life?
The world would split open.
  — Muriel Rukeyser, "Kathe Kollwitz"

Some authors become devoted to a cause and express a combative voice.

What's the use in being a writer if you can't irritate a great
many people?
  — Norman Mailer

Mailer took on American icons such as Marilyn Monroe as well as American politics, even convicted murderers, and succeeded in irritating a great many people, but he had the courage to speak in his own voice. His was one of the many voices raised in protest at the continuing war in Vietnam. The voice of the artist may sometimes be a prophetic Cassandra crying out or a little boy exclaiming that the Emperor has no clothes. And sometimes, the world listens.

Michael Moore, the off-beat documentary filmmaker from Jackson, Michigan, is such a voice. His independent documentary film *Bowling for Columbine* was far from mainstream Hollywood, but managed to win an Oscar, becoming the first documentary to compete at Cannes Film Festival in forty-six years. The film went on to garner 21 million domestic gross, making it the best selling documentary of all time — for two years. Moore's next film, *Farenheit 9-11,* broke this record in its first weekend and went on to set a new record with an amazing 119 million dollars domestic gross.

Moore cries out against violence and lack of gun control in America, and makes us laugh as well. Moore is a satirist, a kind of American Everyman, and people relate to him. We need more like him. In olden days, the court jester would have such a role — to tease the king and expose problems — without losing his head. In following his own voice, Moore re-invented the documentary.

It is natural, in the beginning, to imitate writers you admire or who have influenced your generation. My first play, *Somewhere-in-Between*, was clearly influenced by Samuel Beckett and Eugene Ionesco, whereas a later play, *The Women of Cedar Creek*, bore tribute to Anton Chekhov. This is rather like the student artists often seen in art museums diligently copying a masterwork by Titian or

Vermeer. Norman Mailer was influenced by Ernest Hemingway, Harold Pinter by Samuel Beckett, and so on. Eventually though, you must find your own voice. And, the first place to look for it, is your own past — the more troubled, the better. Many artists come from dysfunctional homes, and, as a kind of soul survival, learn how to channel the wounds.

MEMORY AS RESOURCE

There is no greater resource for a writer than his own memory, both personal and collective. To quote screenwriter David Field (*Amazing Grace and Chuck*):

> Surely remembering a life is a work of unintentional art. The mental hand winnows through runes of memory searching for meaning, patterns, warmth, significance. All is fiction. All is story. All is metaphor.

This holds true not only for autobiography or memoir writing, but for all narrative forms as well. How I remember is how I give meaning to a life lived. One usually remembers in bits and pieces, not wholes. An image, a smell, a sound, a phrase of dialogue spoken may precipitate a flood of memory flushing the portals of the mind.

My first acting teacher was Lee Strasberg at the Actors Studio in New York City. Strasberg had been inspired by his contact with the Moscow Art Theatre and the works of the great Russian actor and teacher, Constantin Stanislavski, as outlined in his book, *An Actor Prepares*. In class, Strasberg would guide us through sense memory and later emotional memory exercises. Briefly, it would begin like this. Imagine you are drinking a cup of coffee at breakfast. How does the cup feel in your hand, the warmth, and so on. The object is to awaken your senses of touch, smell, and sight. Later, emotional recall would be added to the mix. Once the grounding of the senses is there, you would get in touch with whatever memory was associated or awakened by drinking a cup of coffee at breakfast.

Eventually, the actor would use these skills while acting in a scene or a play, thereby infusing the text with his own emotional and sense memories from the past. Of course, the memory details would be private — only the outer effect of the inner work would be seen by the audience.

To apply this to writing, you might write of a character being in love, and spontaneously or consciously engage your own memory of a specific lover or parent — his touch, his voice, and so on. The effect of drawing upon your own memories transforms a fictional story into a believable one. This need not match exactly what you are writing about. Here's an example.

When I wrote the play *On the Edge: The Final Years of Virginia Woolf,* I was stumped how to write the love scene between two women, that is, between Virginia and Vita. After talking with a lesbian friend, I learned that with homosexual couples, one sometimes adopts a male role and the other a female one. So in writing the play, I envisioned Vita as a man and Virginia as a woman. The rest was easy. I simply drew from my own past romance and the residue of stored feelings.

Once I was walking along the Avenue of the Americas in midtown Manhattan amidst towering skyscrapers, and suddenly smelled hay. It was distinct and irrefutable. The odd thing was that the smell preceded the stored memory of hay and a Texas childhood. In Marcel Orphuls' documentary film, *Hotel Terminus*, about Klaus Barbie, the Nazi torturer, one of his victims remembered, as if yesterday, minute details of the traumatic event over forty years before. She recalled what Barbie was wearing, the expression on his face, which parts of her body were tortured. There is a certain mystery about memory as well as a sensual inclusiveness. One is imprinted by memory, even governed by it. No one is exempt from its power — least of all, the writer of story.

Despite its power, memory usually appears as disjointed fragments. These fragments may make no sense at all at first, yet serve to draw us into a labyrinth journey which, if faithfully followed, lead us back to some deeper layer of our psyche. Nobel Laureate Toni Morrison's haunting novel *Beloved* is a superb example of the play and power of memory. To quilt the bits and pieces of her work is to embark on a journey both personal and collective. Toni Morrison says, "Memory ... is a form of willed creation." *Beloved* has been compared to such epic works as Homer's *Odyssey* and Melville's *Moby Dick*. What is amazing is how this inner-reaching story achieves the same epic dimensions as such outer journeys as *The Odyssey* and *Moby Dick*. All three evoke the process and archetypal myths of journey and memory.

In *Moby Dick*, Ishmael turns to the sea to find himself whereas Sethe in *Beloved* turns inward to memory, opting to stay in one room: "The world is in this room. This here's all there is and all there needs to be." The memory of home spurs Odysseus through countless obstacles whereas Sethe's forbidden memories of Sweet Home drive her deeper and deeper into the dark past where she encounters demons of guilt and ghostly, monstrous memories. Sethe's fierce love for her dead baby drives her as surely as does Captain Ahab's obsessive hatred. Both are powerful emotions that can equally render epic proportions. Both characters are wounded by life, yet one ends in self-destruction while the other renews her life. Ahab with his "birthmark... from crown to sole" stands with "a crucifixion in his face," and his end echoes this when he is pinned and crucified to the very object of his hatred, Moby Dick. Seth's wound is the wound and shame of slavery cut into her very flesh — yet this wound resembles not crucifixion but rather a chokeberry tree, symbol of life. Both Ahab and Sethe are marked by wounded memories, yet one character hastens crucifixion and the other, resurrection.

Beloved, Sethe's daughter, is no less real because she is a ghost returned. She is memory made real through the creative process of writing, Sethe's memory dreaming her back into reality. Memory can be creative as well. Beloved returns many years after her death yet rather than return as a baby, she returns as a girl of 18, the very age she would be had she lived. Yet because she has not lived those years, the novelist gives her the emotional traits of a small baby. Hence, Beloved is both the dead baby come back as baby *and* the imagined girl of 18. Beloved has no memory for she is memory. To quote the author: "Beloved, the title character, is created out of memory itself."

The novel is at first confusing, fragmented, illogical — like life. In 1999, when Oprah Winfrey admitted to Toni Morrison how she had to puzzle over her novel, Morrison dryly replied, "That, my dear, is called reading." She not only expects the reader to puzzle, but to plunge whole into her dream play, as this is the only way the fragments can make sense.

One of the confusions is the story not fitting into a narrow linear, psychological container. It is interesting that Oprah Winfrey's movie adaptation of Morrison's novel somehow missed its mark. Perhaps the fault lay in attempting a too literal translation of the book. Also films rely on a prime turning point, after which the life radically changes. Novels often provide more scope wherein life progresses and works in bits and pieces, often turning symbolically in on itself. What happens is not always external. *Beloved* cannot be grasped as a flat-on narrative. What is required is a sideway vision. Here story moves more like a dream than a waking reality.

The challenge and indeed mythic greatness of Morrison's use of memory in her novel is that it is both personal and collective. The visionary work carries the collective unconscious. It is likely that Morrison in the act of writing itself channeled things she could not know, the collective memory pouring through her unconscious fingers. The creative process is a portal to the unknown, gateway to not one but perhaps countless lifetimes. The psychologist, C.G. Jung, once said that "We need not try to determine whether the content of the vision is of a physical, psychic, or metaphysical nature. In itself it has psychic reality, and this is *no less real* than physical reality."

The novel *Beloved* is more than anyone's personal story, it is the story of a people — as epics usually are. It carries the dark shadow of slavery, and yet it is more even than this. This is a novel about *the enslavement of memory itself,* enslavement in the widest universal sense. Again, in Morrison's own words: "The novel turned out to be a composition of parts circling each other, like the galaxy (of emotions) accompanying memory." One must let go of the rational to enter this world, this world where dead babies return fully grown.

The writer or artist, as a modern-day shaman, serves as a go-between or bridge between the two worlds, and memory is inevitably his starting point. The writer is a receptor who, in turn, processes it inwardly and finally spews it forth into its collective shape.

In writing stories, however, it is necessary for the writer to express himself not only through his own voice, but through the voices of his characters. And each voice will have its own point of view.

THE VOICE OF CHARACTER

The following is a true story. A boy of five is asked by his parents if he would give blood to his three-year-old sister who might die without the right blood transfusion. The boy hesitates, then asks if he could decide the next morning. "Of course," his parents agree. The next morning the boy solemnly tells them that yes, he will give his blood to his sister. At the hospital, the little boy is on the gurney near his sister when the doctor comes over to begin the transfusion process. At this point, the little boy looks up at the doctor and asks, "How soon before I die?" This clearly states the boy's point of view. We suddenly experience the whole story through his eyes.

Choosing a story which moves you will provide your point of view (POV), so important in a great story. Your perspective is your voice and mirrors your personal values — unlike no others. How you feel about your characters, story, and/or theme is what makes your story unique. Focus the story by telling it from your character's point of view or perspective. Usually this means from the main character's perspective — but not always. Sometimes a lesser character viewing the great man as in the Italian film, *Il Postino (The Postman)*, a fictional account of the great poet Neruda as seen through the eyes of a village postman in rural Italy. Or Nick in *The Great Gatsby*, both novel and film. Nick is the witness of the story's main action which centers on Gatsby.

How then to find your own voice as a writer? In order to discover your voice as a writer, it is important to explore your own personal myth. Who and what influenced you? What imprints are carried over from early childhood? What wounds? What inspirations? As the popular singer Kenny Loggins once said, "That's what art is, that's what we do. Reveal part of ourselves that we may not want to get into."

Another self-trained singer icon, Joni Mitchell, says she simply found chords which matched her feelings. Style is the way you see yourself and the world about you. Integrity matters, fashion not at all.

To serve as an example, I will attempt the exercise of discovering my own personal myth, and then ask you to do the same.

ONE WOMAN'S JOURNEY

I can remember myself at age seven, sitting outside and watching the long stretch of grassy Texas lawn and an endless driveway dotted with rose bushes, waiting... waiting for someone to come and carry me away to my rightful place. Even as a small child, I knew I did not belong here, that this place was not home. Strange how even when very young, we know where we belong and where we don't. These people were not my people. I was right, though it would be many years before I would find my tribe.

> Coming into this particular body and being born of these particular parents and in such a place, and in general what we call external circumstances. That all happenings form a unity and are spun together is signified by the Fates.
> — Plotinus

At the age of four, we were living in Japan after the war. I remember looking up at a colossal stone Buddha, and pondering, "Oh, this is what they mean by God." The same year I was excited to see for the first time colorful, Japanese actresses dancing at a cherry blossom festival in the park. I ran away because I wanted to join the company. Some hours later I was found and brought home. These two events would foreshadow my particular tension of opposites: the beginning of a religious or spiritual journey intertwined with a love of self-expression through drama. C. G. Jung writes of the tension of opposites: "If (the individual) succeeds in giving collective validity to his widened consciousness, he creates a tension of opposites that provides the stimulation which culture needs for its further progress." Here lies an excellent definition of the artist. It seems also that this tension of opposites propels us into what the Greeks might call our destiny or fate. These two poles would remain for me a spiritual quest for meaning combined with a path of creative expression as purpose. Most times these created a tug of war within, yet once in a while they would merge into some creative form such as a play, film, or book. Stephenson Bond states that "the birth of the personal myth in the imagination of a single individual may become the rebirth of the greater myths in the imagination of the culture." This is simply another way of saying that in the specific lies the universal.

As a teenager, I felt revulsion to a Puritanical minister whose ravings of hell and damnation terrified little children, I broke away from the Southern Baptist Church. My grandmother who lived with us did not speak to me for three weeks. I sought a gentler form of Christianity such as Christ saying, "Suffer the little children…". Joining a more liberal Protestant church, I became youth minister and actually gave a sermon once a year. At seventeen I majored in theology and prepared myself to become an educational missionary. This same year, however, I began outside of class to devour books of the great religions of the world as well as read eastern and western philosophy. This lead to an inner crisis as I realized that God was only a projection of something else, and was in no way limited to one name. Now an agnostic, I turned to my other calling — remember the Japanese dancing girls? Dedicating myself to Thespis, a new god, I changed universities and direction by studying theatre arts in a well-known drama school. I acquired a B.F.A. and would later launch my dramatic career in New York City.

EXERCISE: DISCOVERING YOUR PERSONAL MYTH

As you read the next paragraph, think of a myth or fairytale which speaks to you and serves as a metaphor for your own life's journey. Again, here is an example from my own life, which you may wish to read before writing your own. Just keep in mind what was similar in your own life, or different.

Agnostic or not, my religious search for meaning would not rest. It now caused me to fall in love with a remarkable philosopher/novelist, a Brahmin from south India, a stranger from a strange land. This is why the Greek myth of Ariadne calls to me as a parallel metaphor of my own journey. Ariadne, goddess of Crete, mistress of the labyrinth, fell in love at first sight and risked all, including her own birthright, to serve and follow a stranger from a strange land. She became for her lover, Theseus, a guide to the underworld. Her gift of the golden thread was an offering of her self. She would not be the last woman to give away all for love. Having forsaken home and family, she was in turn abandoned by her lover, her god, victim perhaps from her own sleep of romantic illusion. This abandonment, however, marked the beginning of growth and transformation so necessary before being chosen by a higher god, Dionysus. He, in turn, made her his bride of death which might be interpreted as a final stage in transformation.

This particular Ariadne hailed from Texas, a descendant of Davy Crockett whose own passion for freedom ended in his death in the defense of the Alamo. The tendency to project ideals onto causes or quests persists. After the rather intense bout of religion already described, I fell away from religion and embraced a quest for Truth. It was the mid-sixties in America. You either marched in Selma or turned toward the east for answers. After dallying with civil rights, I embraced the latter. India appeared in the form of a remarkable Brahmin novelist/philosopher from south India, Raja Rao (*The Serpent and the Rope*), nominated for the Nobel Literary Prize, who came to the university to speak of eastern philosophy. He was fifty-five and I was nineteen. And my heart leaped at first sight of him. I would be his muse, his anima, his thread through life's labyrinth, his love. Soon, I would become his wife and the mother of our son. Opposed to our union, my conservative Texas family came after my Theseus at gunpoint — Texas style — and we escaped and were wed in Paris, the mythic city of love. Later I would embrace my husband's land, India, which would prove a catalyst for deep, inner change. The many years lived there by the sacred river Pampa were indeed a blessing of the gods. I see now that this time away from life as usual became a foundation of all that was to follow. Stripped of all that was familiar to me, it enabled me to sink deeper into myself, welcoming new gods. India is a mirror which intensifies whatever is reflected in one's self. This wonder that is India shall ever remain deep in the inner geography of my journey. As David Miller says in his excellent book, *The New Polytheism,* "The ancient divinities live on through us and we play out their stories." Which story or myth are you playing out? Begin to form your own parallels or contrasts as you continue to read the following.

My life, as many, has been full of sudden shifts. As a child, I was Persephone lost in an underworld of darkness. I grew through motherhood, as Demeter, awakening to the fierce force of maternal love. There were reclusive years in a small ashram in India followed by Dionysian years performing in the New York theatre.

The way back to Self is not an easy journey but the only one worth making. As a woman, I came to realize it was not my soul's purpose to help another through the labyrinth but to thread my own way back to Self. I finally left a marriage which almost claimed me as a bride of death to my own individuality. Somehow this Ariadne emerged to discover in the end that she is no longer separate from what she sought. I walk in the void of not-knowing as forms fall away like snake skins. To view one's life symbolically and not literally is to discover meaning at each and every step. It is a never-ending story. Myth is both personal and collective. Though individual in detail, the archetypal patterns are universal, ever changing, and unlike dogma or religion, its forms are as varied and as changeless as the sea. What matters is to discover your own personal myth, what you care strongly about, and write with that voice.

EXERCISE: WRITE YOUR PERSONAL MYTH

What myth or fairy tale or icon do you identify with? Snow White? Marilyn Monroe? Robinson Crusoe? First briefly describe the mythic story, then what in your life connects with it. Write in the first person, and let it be as long as it needs to be. You might begin, "I remember myself at age __ when..."

The 2003 National Book Awards gave its highest honor to Stephen King, a master storyteller. There had been controversy over this decision as King is considered not a literary writer but a popular writer. As were Charles Dickens and Victor Hugo, I might add. King writes horror stories and this was considered outside the literary arena. What did they think Edgar Allen Poe wrote? (Poe, incidentally, created a new genre called mystery, pre-dating *Sherlock Holmes*.) Walter Mosley, in presenting the award to King, spoke of how Stephen King's stories are anchored in the experience of the ages, and cited Mark Twain and Nathaniel Hawthorne. The point in citing this here is that King, who came from a working-class background, wrote from his own perspective, his own voice. He did not try and write like other writers. He remains true to his own background and to the inner world of his unique imagination. And he is a born storyteller.

Someone remarked the ships and landscapes that nineteenth-century William Turner painted were not accurate, to which the English artist replied, "I am interested in drawing what I see, not what I know."

Intention and purpose are needed to create a vision. Director and screenwriter, Anthony Minghella, spoke at the Getty Art Museum in Los Angeles: "The job of the artist is not to document but to conjure, to create a story more true than what is true. What has meaning is an emotional truth, not literal truth."

When painters in the early thirties and forties were flocking to Paris, Georgia O'Keefe stayed in America and painted what she felt. In this way, she found her voice.

> I paint what I see, only larger.
> — Georgia O'Keeffe

Someone said of Claude Monet that he was only an eye. Edouard Manet remarked, "Yes, but what an eye!" Vincent Van Gogh once painted a simple yellow chair that he had in his studio. Here, an ordinary object was transformed into a great vision by the artist's perspective.

Subjectivity is necessary for all art, especially writing. Just as the painter paints from a specific perspective, so must the writer. He must stand someplace in order to put forth his particular, unique vision.

As I write this chapter, I hear on the radio news that Spalding Gray, actor and monologist, is dead at sixty-two. He jumped from the Staten Island Ferry, committing suicide, as did his mother years before. A tragic loss. With Gray's one-man play and later film, *Swimming to Cambodia*, Gray found his own subjective form.

> Creativity is harnessing universality and making it flow through your eyes.
> — Peter Koestenbaum

There are as many points of views as there are writers. A somewhat unusual example is poet Stephen Todd Booker, a condemned murderer on Death Row since the age of twenty-five. He is now fifty and acclaimed for his poetry. Unable to see the stars for a period of twelve years, he began to write about them from the perspective of a bat.

Harper Lee wrote one novel, a novel of her childhood. Another Southern child was her friend Truman Capote, who became the prototype for one of the children in the novel. The novel, *To Kill a Mockingbird*, became a classic film which starred Gregory Peck in his finest performance. The novel is written from the perspective of a young girl coming of age in the South. Carson McCullers, another Southern writer, summoned her childhood memories in the novel, play, and film, *A Member of the Wedding*, starring a very young and luminous Julie Harris. We hear the ache of a lonely young girl wanting to belong to someone, somewhere. McCullers displays her unique voice in such memorable lines as, "The we of me."

Finding Nemo (2003), the Disney animated film, provides another compelling example of point of view. Marlin (voiced by Albert Brooks), a father fish, struggles with parental fears and over-protectiveness when his handicapped son Nemo, with an undersized flipper, becomes lost. Anyone who has ever been a child or a parent will relate to this character. As Marlin faces danger upon danger on the journey to find his son, he faces and overcomes his own fears.

Again, it is the *feeling* which is communicated to the reader and audience, enabling us to identify with the writer's journey. No clever tricks here — so rampant in today's market — only heart-felt originality.

No bird soars too high if he soars with his own wings.
— William Blake

It is no coincidence that many of our best writers, like Jack London and John Steinbeck, did an assortment of jobs and experienced life, before sitting down to write. This was also true of Blaise Cendras, the now classic French author, who said, "I dip my pen not in ink, but in life."

One example of the subjective voice is that of my maternal grandmother who grew up on a farm in north Texas. She was sharing her past with me one rainy afternoon, describing how people would share their crops with one another during the Depression. "Oh," I said, "you mean you bartered." "No," she replied firmly, "We gave, and they gave." Her point of view was quite different from that of my own generation. With these simple words, she enabled me to see the past with her eyes. And her perspective had more heart.

Tom Eidson, who wrote the Western novel, *The Missing,* later adapted into a film starring Cate Blanchett and Tommy Lee Jones, said, "I know about tragic alienation among family members. It's kind of a personal story. It's not accurate in factual history but in emotional history."

There is perhaps no better example of a personal subjective voice in literature than America's own Mark Twain. Twain, whose real name was Samuel Clemens, wrote as though there was no literature before him. He observed, listened, then with local American language, turned it into the literature of *Huckleberry Finn* or *The Mysterious Stranger.* The now-classic *Huckleberry Finn* opens with a monologue in the voice of the title character, Huck Finn. Through this voice, we enter Huck's world. Twain began the novel with the voice. Once he found the voice, the story seems to tell itself. When the personal voice meets the universal, a classic is born. Here is Huck's opening monologue:

> You don't know about me without you have read a book by the name of *The Adventures of Tom Sawyer,* but that ain't no matter. That book was made by Mr. Mark Twain, and he told the truth, mainly.

Note the mark of Twain's genius with the last word "mainly." Twain quite cleverly has his main character introduce the book, establishing at once a connection between Huck and the reader. The journey has begun, and it is an intimate one.

While Hawthorne and Melville were patterning their works on English classics, Twain who left school at age twelve, wrote from life, an American life. Mark Twain cared deeply about certain themes and issues such as slavery and boldly airs his views in Huckleberry Finn. (Incidentally, due to Twain's outspoken views on anti-slavery, the book was banned for several years in America.)

> The weight of this sad time we must obey. Speak what we feel, not what we ought to say.
> — William Shakespeare, *King Lear*

Charles Dickens adapts the same approach with the opening lines of *David Copperfield*:

> Whether I shall turn out to be the hero of my own life, or whether that station will be held by anybody else, these pages must show. To begin my life with the beginning of my life, I record that I was born...

As does Charlotte Bronte in *Jane Eyre*, giving readers a new appreciation for the gothic novel as literature. At the close of the novel, Bronte writes as though she is writing an intimate letter to a friend. it is Jane Eyre's voice and it is Charlotte Bronte's voice as well, "Reader, I married him. A quiet wedding we had: he and I...." And later on, she continues:

> I have now been married ten years. I know what it is to live entirely for and with what I love best on earth... No woman was ever nearer to her mate than I am: ever more absolutely bone of his bone and flesh of his flesh.

First we must care in order for the reader or audience to care. The way to caring is by creating a character the reader or audience can identify with which enables them to emotionally connect. This is the magic that compels you tell someone they must read this book or see this movie. It is always feeling which generates enthusiasm.

Home is where you tell your secrets. Story is where writer and audience (or reader) meet because they need one another. For a moment in time, we come together in an experience more real than any other.

> Art is a way that you tell the world around you how you see things. It's a way for you to reflect back to the world.
> — Bille August, Danish film director

No matter what you are writing about, you must find a way to write about it. And for this, you must find a personal voice.

In *Remembrance of Things Past*, French writer Marcel Proust conquered Time in autobiography by exploring the self. He invented nothing, but altered everything. He did this by finding his own unique voice. Proust wrote no epic, he simply confined his writing to what he could perceive from his bed. An asthmatic, Proust was mostly confined to bed, where he wrote, and relied on the gossip of his housekeeper and friends.

Writing in the third person can also explore the soul of a character. Here is a contemporary example:

> Her stories grew and changed as she tested them... but all of them started from a core of what she knew and sensed about people. And it was not even that she made up anything but rather that she listened closely to herself.
> — Ursula Hegi, *Stones from the River*

A few years ago, I was a guest professor at a graduate school in a respected university. A student came to me and confided that he had been told by his professor — a known writer from New York City — that he should quit writing. Why? Because this first-time instructor — who was invited to teach based on her success as a short story writer — expected the students to write as she did. I cringe when I hear such stories. Unfortunately, they are not as uncommon as they should be. The young man went on to say that he had decided to try one more writing class before giving up writing for good. And this young man was the best writer in my class! He wrote in a fantasy style — quite different from the New Yorker's more realistic style.

To preserve individuality and save it from herd-like conformity is one of education's most important challenges.
— Margaret H. Doublery

As a teacher and writing consultant, my goal is to try and see with the eyes of my students or clients. The challenge is to help them fulfill their vision — not mine. I don't think of teaching as simply putting facts into a student's mind, rather it is creating a space for creativity to occur — which might not otherwise happen. There is a huge market today in writing programs and workshops. I can only hope they dedicate themselves to freeing and protecting the individual vision.

> You almost feel that any idiot with a nickel's worth of talent can emerge from a writing class able to write a competent story. In fact, so many people can now write competent stories that the short story as a medium is in danger of dying of competence. We want competence, but competence by itself is deadly. What is needed is the vision to go with it, and you do not get this from a writing class.
> — Flannery O'Connor

Whether you attend classes or not, what matters is to listen to your own voice. It never lies. Hold on to what makes you unique.

> Don't compromise yourself. You're all you've got.
> — Janis Joplin

Chapter 10

Transcending Writer's Block

When the tank runs dry, you have only to leave it alone and it will fill up again.
— Mark Twain

CREATIVE PEOPLE ARE committed to risk. Sometimes the risk is not to write for a period of time. This takes tremendous courage and a certain faith in the creative process.

Contrary to current attitudes, I believe that so-called writer's block is not a malady to be remedied, but rather an opportunity to go deeper. I also believe this is true about depression — unless of course it becomes life threatening. Sometimes depression is simply a signal for change. This might mean a life change such as moving to another city, leaving a marriage, changing careers, or altering one's spiritual path. Rather than suppress the symptom of depression with pharmaceuticals, perhaps it is better to first look more closely, and listen to what it is trying to tell us. In the case of depression accompanying writers block, it might be a signal to write differently, or attempt another theme or form.

These transitions in life and work are usually difficult as is letting go of habits of thinking which no longer serve. Sometimes the block or depression might even be a signal not to write for a while. Not writing is sometimes part of the writing process. As for myself, as with most profound lessons, I had to learn the hard way. All too often, I have made myself suffer needlessly rather than simply accept that it was more important sometimes not to work, to let go for a while the notion of being always outwardly productive. In this way, the real has sufficient time to crystallize.

> The fearful dependence on success is crippling to creation.
> — Harold Clurman

To illustrate, I will relate a true story... my story, as it happens. After seeing several of my plays produced and garner awards, I was surprised at the emptiness I was experiencing. I had become a professional writer and had, somewhere along the line, lost the joy of it — presumably the reason one begins writing in the first place. A change was needed. So I set out on my own to Cornwall, England — home of my Celtic ancestors — to walk the coastal paths, and hopefully, replenish the well. There I experienced a kind of epiphany. After walking a long way out from the village of Mousehole (where poet Dylan Thomas honeymooned and was inspired to write his play, *Under Milkwood*), I came upon a breath-taking view from a Cornish cliff of the restless Atlantic. I stopped to take in the sheer beauty of it. At this precise moment, a thrush perched just a few inches away, opened its beak wide, and began to sing loudly. I turned my head and marveled how this small bird could make such a great and glorious sound. Then, inexplicably, I began to weep. The thrush kept on singing, not minding my emotional display. Why was I weeping? Perhaps because I envied that songbird who sang for the sheer, natural joy of singing — not for agents or critics. This small bird had in one glorious instant taught me an important lesson. One must be one's self, heedless of the world's response. This reminds me of a wonderful cartoon in the *New Yorker* some years ago. It depicts a small bird singing in a tree and instructing a man below. The caption reads, "I don't sing because I'm happy. I'm happy because I sing."

Hope is the thing with feathers
That perches in the soul,
And sings the tune without words,
And never stops at all.
    — Emily Dickinson

In 1866, a publisher rejected the poems of Emily Dickinson, and offered to teach her grammar. Dickinson politely refused the tutorial offer, and continued to write only for herself. Later, after the poet's death, her poems were discovered wrapped in a carefully sewn parcel, hidden under the carpet.

Getting there is going there.
The journey is all, not the destination.
    — Emily Dickinson

When invited to lecture at Skidmore University on any topic, I chose "Art as Process, Not Product" and warned how the commercialism of focusing exclusively on product had harmed American culture. I spoke of how the artist must see his life and work as a journey and a process rather than merely a consumer product. I think I cited van Gogh, who never sold a painting though now his work commands millions of dollars. Now, twenty-five years later, I still believe this, for risk and change matter tremendously — to art as well as for the individuation of the personal life.

I have chosen the way of risk. Often this meant lean and hungry periods while turning down lucrative writing jobs that I could not, in good conscience, accept. I once lost a powerful agent when I refused to accept a lucrative job as staff writer for a successful one-hour prime time drama. Instead I took a job writing an art film in Europe. My values were out of sync with those of Hollywood and as this gap widened, I faced some hard choices: play the game or damage the career. Of course, this is always an individual decision. I can only speak for myself. Even long ago, it seemed better to opt for the way of being true to one's self, even though what seems right one day may change — and usually does. Life is a package deal; one cannot order Life and ask that the hard portions be left out, please. And please know that success can be every bit as dangerous as failure. This seeming crisis became a turning point, opening a new life with greater purpose and meaning.

It was ten years after the Cornwall epiphany, and though a successful screenwriting career in Hollywood had transpired, the feeling of emptiness once again overtook me in spite of, or perhaps because of, the outer success. Little by little, I found myself lost in a labyrinth without Ariadne's thread to find my way back.

I have been fortunate and worked quite a bit in television and film though not everything I have written has been produced — as is usual in Hollywood. Even so, fewer and fewer of the films I was contracted to write were the deeper story ideas I felt passionate about, even if they were my own original ideas. I had learned to write to sell. After completing *Unlikely Angel* and an episode for *Touched by an Angel* starring Olympia Dukakis, I flew to India, and suffered the heat stroke that marked the beginning of what I perceive now as my cave or underworld years. Curiously, the heat stroke seemed a predictable extension of the burnout experienced in Hollywood. This soul-retrieving inner journey took four years, heralding a series of changes in my life, both inner and outer. The outer calamity became, in time, a blessing in disguise.

> My barn having burned down,
> I can now see the moon.
>   — Zen saying

I could no longer live my life in separate parts. I could no longer limit myself to academic lectures exclusively on the craft of writing as I had done for many years. The urge to be whole was overwhelming. I knew beyond doubt that my approach to both writing and teaching others to write had to be a holistic and integrative approach.

> If you build it, they will come.
>   — W. P. Kinsella, *Shoeless Joe* (novel made into the film *Field of Dreams*)

For four years I did not write. I could not write. Feeling pressure from agents and producers, I would make sincere attempts, yet weird occurrences would stall me. Twice I tried to push the river, forcing myself to write. Here is what happened. The first time, I fell and fractured my right wrist. (Yes, I am right-handed.) The second time I exerted my will — snap out of it and just do it — my computer, only a year old, blew. By then, the message was clear: it was not yet time to write. I was forced, from the outside, to attend to the inner changes going on. By now, I felt rather like an obstinate mule that has to be given a hard whack in order to get her attention! Something deep within was trying to get my attention all right, and I had no choice but to attend. Without this journey, this book would not have been born, and my life — which has become richer — would not have been.

The way through is acceptance, not resistance. The unconscious has a way of going its own way, so best to opt for the path of least resistance, and follow it.

In older cultures, shamans often healed by re-connecting the person to his soul, which has, through some loss or trauma, become disconnected. I suspect this is as true today as when the practice began. We live in a time of fragmentation, and should be open to the invisibles to help restore balance. I had admittedly become a workaholic, and it was and continues to be a long process toward wholeness.

> If you want to work on your art, work on your life.
> — Anton Chekhov

Robert Fritz, in his article, "Living Dead and the Holy Redeemed," speaks of the danger of falling into traps of deadness:

What once was real can become empty form. We can find ourselves, little by little, becoming numb, mindless, and dull, going through the motions. And all the time, we might not know we are drifting into such deadness. What makes a theater a living theater is that it is still exploring, inventing, creating, searching, reaching, aspiring, fully in touch with its vision and fully in touch with reality as it is and as it changes. In the arts, it is common knowledge that form without substance kills the spirit. And no one sets out to create spiritless forms. But artists are human beings, and they too, their training and profession notwithstanding, can slip into deadening form. It's when they stop reaching for something new, stop creating something fresh and original, and begin to fall back on techniques and tricks rather than on truth and originality that the performance becomes a dead and empty form. It's not the actual forms in our lives that are deadening us. It is losing touch with the holiness of life. Each moment has a potential for renewal by being new. This is the essence of the creative process, and why so many creators have more life per square inch than do many other people. They must be in touch with the reality of the moment, the source of their visions, the relationship with life that comes from finding something new, vital, meaningful, real, substantive, and transcendent.

It took four long years to recover my health from the heat stroke suffered in India, and to reconnect to my soul's journey. Something within shifted, as did my outer life. I did other things than writing: community service organizing cultural events and various international speakers in philosophy and alternative medicine. Time with friends and family became more important. I considered a second marriage, but shied away at the last minute. In short, I shed my strong identity as a writer, and got a life.

Tony and Academy Award–winning director Mike Nichols commented in a Los Angeles interview, "There's something about not doing something that lets it grow inside you. You're saying, 'I'm not a career. I'm a person'."

> What we play is life.
> — Louis Armstrong

I have noticed over the years that my dreams are far richer when I am not writing. Once I am writing again, they seem to subside, as if, during waking hours, my dream story images are already flowing into the project at hand. So, during this fallow time, my dreams became a channel for a creative life gone underground, as it were. I wrote them down. I listened to their messages. I worked with the dream images which became presences and guides through the dark periods. Balance was needed, and once I opened to the real inner work, the unconscious became my guide. Synchronicities began to appear to guide me.

In a dark time, the eye begins to see.
— Theodore Roethke

One dream which came was of a woman who was five months pregnant. This signaled a new beginning four months from now. Yet I did not know what. I trusted that if I remained open, the "what" would appear. And it did. Invited to speak at a film conference, it was suggested that I meet a colleague who was also invited and happened to live near me. We had lunch and she told me she was attending Pacifica Graduate Institute in Santa Barbara, California, studying Mythology. The intuitive inner voice seemed to activate, and I somehow knew this was my next step. What I am saying is the very word Pacifica created an intuitive response and I simply knew. The next graduate sessions began in September — the ninth month — four months away. I immediately phoned the Institute and learned that the next day was the final day to register. Without reading a catalogue or asking anything, I made the 40-minute drive from my home to Pacifica Graduate Institute in Santa Barbara. Then, after 20 years of teaching, I cut back, doing book reviews and consultant work instead. This began a two-year journey studying Mythology and Depth Psychology (Jungian and post-Jungian psychology). What it really was, however, was a journey back to Self.

It was comforting to read in C. G. Jung's autobiography *Memories, Dreams, and Reflections*, that after breaking away from Sigmund Freud, he underwent a period of confusion for four years. He left his academic post and did little outwardly from the age of 37 to 41 — a period of uncertainty and inner change. He gave himself over to images of psyche and the unconscious. Later he remarked that what was to become his life work was based on the discoveries of these four lost years.

> The years when I was pursuing my inner images were the most important in my life — in them everything essential was decided.
> — C. G. Jung

There is also the example of the great Austrian poet, Rainer Maria Rilke, who for ten years wrote nothing due to an inner crisis, then traveled to Italy, and within ten days, composed the *Duino Elegies*:

> Here is the time for the sayable
> here is its home.
> Speak, bear witness. More than ever
> things fall away from us
> livable things and what crowds them out
> and replaces them
> is an event for which there's no image.
>   — Rainer Maria Rilke ("The Ninth Elegy," translated by
>   David Young)

Later I spoke with friend and colleague Cecil Dawkins (*The Quiet Enemy*), the short story writer and novelist. Dawkins taught writing at Sarah Lawrence College not far from where I taught at The New School University, until she suddenly left New York City for New Mexico. I shared with Cecil the blunt truth that I had not written in four years, and was amazed at her response! "That's nothing. I didn't write for fourteen years!" She went on to tell me that instead, she built a house, literally built it herself. She said this time in New Mexico saved her, changing her life in the process. Then she said, "The artist must stay true to herself." (Many of Flannery O'Connor's letters are written to Cecil Dawkins, who was a close friend of O'Connor's, and are now published as *The Letters of Flannery O'Connor*.)

So, after teaching others for twenty years, I was about to return to school myself by returning to graduate school. Obviously, becoming a student in a different subject was not a shrewd career move. This was not an MBA, after all. My practical Texas family asked, "But what do you intend to do with a graduate degree in Mythology?" I replied, "It's not what I will do with mythology, but what mythology will do with me."

So this certainly was not a career move, as such, but rather a movement towards soul. Uncertain as it was, somehow I knew from within that it was right — even if I did not yet know why. I decided once again to simply trust the process. I knew without knowing that if I could hold the chaos churning within, that one day it would be transformed into a dancing star.

> The future is uncertain but this uncertainty is at the very heart
> of human creativity.
>   — Ilya Prigogine, Nobel Prize–winning physicist

For me, a playwright and screenwriter, the uncertainty was to
alter the way I taught writing, and to eventually write this book.
Stuck in my habitual track of writing plays and Hollywood films, I
could not see doing anything else. I could not see it simply because
I had never done it before. So Life had to intervene and shake
me so that the necessary inner work prepared the new way — an
empty space for something entirely new to emerge. Another boon
of attending graduate school was that I had to write many, many
long papers, thereby developing a prose style — quite different
than writing dialogue and stage directions! (This week, when a
friend asked how writing this book was going, I joked, "It's hard.
In screenplays, I don't have to fill up the whole page!")

By letting go of my identity as a professional writer and as a
professor of writing, by becoming a student again, I found my way
back. There is something powerful and humbling about letting go
of everything and starting over. Though certainly a risk, it is a true
adventure of the soul.

> Creativity can be described as letting go of certainties.
>   — Gail Sheehy, *Passages*

What is important, I think, is to trust the process of the inner
journey. And, writing, if it has integrity, is an inner journey. It
takes courage to be open and risk all for the truth of the moment
and to remain open to change. One of the meanings of "change"
is to transform. What if the intention in life became less utilitarian
and more transforming? More open to growth and change. Then
wherever we go, whatever it is we do, we do consciously, and with
purpose.

> We learn by going where we have to go.
>   — Theodore Roethke

If this is so, one must allow for the shadow or empty periods
which inevitably arise for some unknown reason, when to understand might demand time.

Clouds come from time to time and bring to men a chance to
rest from looking at the moon.
— Basho

The will can only carry the creative person so far. At some point,
you must make yourself ready, and surrender to a higher consciousness. Trust the inner process. Writing, like life, is a spiritual journey,
a journey through dark forests as well as sunny landscapes.

The poet Cynthia Ozick defines writing as essentially an act of
courage. Of course, this is so. However, sometimes not writing is
an act of courage as well.

The key to healing, as well as writing the best you can, is self-
acceptance. It can be a turning point to accept that this may be
a dormant time necessary for your inner growth. Farmers understand that land needs replenishing, to be left dormant for one or
two years, before planting. Human souls are the same.

Several years ago, I was invited, as a playwright, to the Wurlitzer
Foundation in Taos, New Mexico, for a month's retreat in order
to write, undisturbed. It was a welcome change from living near
Times Square in New York City. What followed was unexpected,
however. I met some artists who were also invited to stay there.
They gave me supplies and I began to paint for the first time in
my life. (I was the child who got out of art classes in order to
spend more time in the library.) So I began to draw with pencil
and chalk, then to do water colors of the splendid Taos landscapes.
Also, I hiked daily in the mountains which had a special energy.
After two weeks of this, I began to feel guilty as I had been invited
there to write — and was not writing. So I told the director that I
was hiking and drawing and painting instead. Imagine my relief
when he said, "I don't care. It's your time. Do what you want." So
I allowed myself to explore other disciplines.

It was only sometime later that I realized what the drawing
and painting had done for me, as a writer. It taught me to see in an
entirely different way. You must see detail if you draw anything,
dimensions, shading, etc. I have never painted again after that
summer in Taos, yet the gift of seeing more deeply has remained.

Perhaps today we have become over-specialized, believing we
must only be one thing, only do one thing in order to succeed.

Arthur Miller once told me a true story which is an excellent example of the danger of over-specialization. Miller was flying from New York to Los Angeles and happened to be sitting next to a scientist. As they flew over the Mohave Desert, the scientist pointed out that his people had discovered that they could bring water to this wasteland by simply dropping a bomb there. Miller asked, "But wouldn't that harm the air?" The scientist replied, "Oh, that's not my field."

Perhaps it is necessary to state that I do not lessen the importance of singular focus in order to achieve anything, at various periods in a writing life. And I am not advocating self-indulgently doing nothing for most of your life. I do not mean giving up or simply passively not writing. Quite the contrary. It is very important to remain receptive to what is going on. Apart from keeping a dream journal, journaling can be very helpful during the shadow or dormant times. Perhaps a *Way of Story* group or other support groups can fill the gap. Reading is important. To write well one must read well. And it can also be helpful to do inner practices such as meditation or long solitary walks or sitting in a garden in order to listen to inner directives.

> Stay at your table and listen. Don't even listen, just wait, be completely quiet and alone. The world will offer itself to you to be unmasked.
> — Franz Kafka

Sometimes writers — both professional and amateur — simply need to return to Self, to get in touch with that small still center from where all good writing emerges. As Pulitzer Prize–winning playwright August Wilson writes in *Joe Turner's Come and Gone*, "See, Mr. Loomis, when a man forgets his song he goes off in search of it... till he find out he's got it with him all the time." This reminds me of the climactic scene in *The Wizard of Oz* when the heroes learn that each of them already possesses what they were looking for in the first place.

Sometimes, changing directions in life and work, then creating an empty space within and without, is what is required. And then being still, listening for guidance.

To the mind that is still, the world surrenders.
— Lao Tzu

If you are faithful to the inner process, you will know when it is time to return to writing. It will occur in spite of you.

And then, out of many years of silence and failure and feeling that my whole life was a disaster, the writing came, like a blessing, like a door that opened into another space.
— Isabel Allende

Once the decision to write again is taken, it is vital to allow scheduled time to sit at the table or desk or before your computer. Just sit facing the blank page or screen. Then write whatever comes to mind, as free association or a journaling process. The rest will follow in its own time — if not in your time. Writing, like other important relationships, requires attention and patience.

EXERCISE: FAVORITE WORDS

Just for fun, take a blank sheet of paper (not computer) and allow yourself to be completely still. Look at the paper as though you were reading it. Then, in your own sweet time, begin to write down favorite words — words which have meaning for you. (Some of my favorites are pilgrim soul, spiritual, journey, home, child, awe.) After you have a short list, pick one of the words and begin to write down all your associations with it. Let it take you where it will. Images. Memories. Perhaps a new idea for a story.

Guard against self-criticism, for it is the least helpful at this stage. During my years of not-writing regularly, my innate Puritan work ethic was the most deadly, as well as the internalized parent's voice. It caused me to mistakenly try and force instead of surrendering to the process. If this occurs, then set yourself small writing tasks — perhaps writing three pages daily in your journal. Don't think on it, don't judge it — just do it. Creativity is the only cure for criticism. Set small and gentle goals and meet them.

Sometimes, spontaneous surprises may come, gifting you. For instance, I was asked by a magazine to write an article on the theme of *Life Changes*. Several writers were asked to write on this theme and encouraged to be as honest and revealing as possible. I wrote about the heat stroke and the shadow years, and how this period changed my life for the better. Then unexpectedly, I was invited to Zacca Lake, California for a private retreat. It so happened that there was also a conference of shamans there for a weekend workshop. And though I was not a participant in their conference, we had our meals together. There I met a female shaman from Canada who later inspired my short story, "The Woman Who Talked to Stones." It was later published in a literary journal, the *El Dorado Sun*. When I say I did not write for four years, I meant I was not sitting down daily at my desk as I had for the last two decades. I had not planned to write this story, you see, it simply came through. A gift.

So staying open, writing in a journal, reading, recording dreams, arranging solitary quiet times are all part of the writing process, even if you are not writing in the sense you once imagined it. Harold Clurman wrote in his wonderful book, *All People Are Famous*, "They should realize, these impatient ones, that often what one gathers on the path to accomplishment is more rewarding than the goal itself."

To work with a living legend is not always a gift, but in this case, it was. What stays with me as I look back on that experience some twenty-five years ago is Clurman's unabashedly boyish enthusiasm for the theatre. He had been directing plays professionally for over forty years when I met and worked with him. Yet he approached my play with the excitement of a man beginning his career, as though nothing in the world were more important than this play. This was the same director who had launched Tennessee Williams, Clifford Odets, and Carson McCuller! Now four decades later, he had somehow retained the love and enthusiasm of a twenty-year-old! Thank you, Harold!

> Success is going from failure to failure without loss of enthusiasm.
> — Winston Churchill

Sometimes a critical failure or crippling reviews will stunt a writer's work. Tennessee Williams said it well, when he defined critics as "eunuchs at the orgy. They can look but they can't do."

By now, I hope the theme of this chapter is clear: It is the journey that matters, not the destination. Yes, "render unto Caesar" when you must so that bills and mortgages are paid. Yet, learn to trust the Self. Trust the inner voice. Trust the process even if it seems mysterious and full of uncertainty. In the final count, it will not let you down.

> Do you have the patience to wait until your mud settles and the water is clear? Can you remain unmoving until the right action arises by itself?
> — Lao Tzu

Looking back on the last years, I cannot but believe that there is an overall plan to each life. Seeming setbacks become doors of perceiving something deeper, wider. Of course, at the time, this knowledge is not usually granted. Something within might know, but not the conscious mind. So you endure the trials. Keep your soul's lamp lit and fueled. Be kind to yourself. In time, your way — there is no one way — will become clear. Meanwhile, while you are waiting, keep learning. Research those topics you feel passionate about. Read. Live. Think. Feel. Love.

> I am always learning.
> — Goya, age ninety-two

It continues to amaze me that most people approach life as though it were a rational process when it so rarely is. One woman who recently took the *Way of Story* workshop mentioned moving to a new town for a job which failed, yet she met the man who would become her husband and soul mate. Now she understands the real reason she moved to this particular town. So the creative process is as true about life as it is about creative work. Now happily married, this same woman has the freedom to write without the commercial pressures of earning a living. Make your life and work from one single cloth: Self.

Each man, each woman, walks a different path. And though it may not make sense from another's perspective, only that individual will know their authentic path. For this, it is imperative to listen within and follow not the world's dictates alone, but that of Soul.

Fame is fleeting for all. Only Soul remains.

Chapter 11

The Way of Story as a Life Path

To write is an act of love. If it is not so, it is only writing.
— Jean Cocteau

PERHAPS IT IS time to return to a cult of Mystery when we think about the creative process and not dissect what is sacred or flatten the living muse through undue picking — as is rampant in many academic institutions, writing conferences, and workshops today. The best teachers — like writers — serve as shamans bridging the two worlds for creativity to emerge and manifest.

In my experience, there is no neat formula for creative success. The little bugger keeps changing on you. Yes, craft matters as earlier explored, but it can never, ever replace the Source of creativity which lies deep within each individual. Why measure a miracle? Allow the process to flow. And above all, try not to separate creative work from life. The general neurosis of our time is that we are split, lacking what is essential: a spiritual connection. To write from one part of your self, the logical mind, results in a fragmented story as well as a fragmented life.

While there is no guarantee that a single-minded devotion to this process will result in career or monetary success, therein lays the magic. For example, I relate an unexpected experience I had some years ago, if only to demonstrate that there must be someone up there looking after the creative fools of this world.

I had not been working in Hollywood long when I was invited to a friend's house for lunch. Sitting on my right was a Finnish film director — though I did not know it at the time. We spoke of philosophy — which is my passion and turned out to be his as well. I shared with him the years I had spent in India studying the Advaita Vedanta philosophy with a great sage. Though I rarely speak of this as it is deeply personal, it seemed natural to do so in this instance. Only at the end of the luncheon did he reveal that he was a film director. Tavi went on to explain that he had come to Hollywood for one purpose: to find a screenwriter who was spiritual.

A few weeks later, during my annual spiritual retreat in South India, a young Indian boy on a bicycle rode out to my small, remote village and delivered a telegram from this same Finnish film director/producer, asking to hire me to adapt the Finnish classic novel, *Wolfbride,* into a screenplay. While meditating seven thousand miles away, I got a job.

In case you haven't guessed by now, I believe in destiny. One can either work with it or fight it. Having done both, I would recommend tuning in, listening, then following the path of least resistance, already there.

I was sometimes dismayed when teaching in what is considered by many to be the number one graduate film school in America. Young writers in their twenties, before completing their first screenplay, possessed an undue focus on how to find an agent. Many — thankfully, not all — of these beginning writers were eager to discover what "they" (the market) wanted, and would inevitably draft a lesser imitation of the latest hit thriller — afterwards becoming confused when it didn't sell! I feel sad when a writer in his twenties is not prepared to risk creatively. If not when you're young, then when?

> All the great things are done for their own sake.
> — Robert Frost

I should add that even when you try and write what the studios want at any given time, what they want will inevitably shift — usually after you've spent several weeks or months writing your script. Then suddenly an original screenplay like *The Sixth Sense* emerges and becomes a hit — and then *that's* what all the studios want — for about two weeks, until the next surprise hit comes out. So by the time you have written your derivative story, the fashion has probably altered.

After several years of living in Los Angeles, I moved to a quieter place, resigned from teaching at the #1 film school, and began presenting *The Way of Story* workshops first at the Esalen Institute in Big Sur, then throughout the States and abroad. My aim was to launch an alternative approach to writing, an approach that valued craft yet served soul.

> We shall require a substantially new manner of thinking if humankind is to survive.
> — Albert Einstein

At the Esalen Institute and elsewhere, I found those receptive to this alternative approach to writing. Unlike students in university classes, most of the workshop participants are no longer in their twenties, but have borne the slings and arrows of the world, and feel a keen need to return to Soul or Self. Only then will they find the necessity and courage to write about what they really care about — and in so doing, heal the split many feel today, both personally and collectively. It is wonderful to teach those who know what they want to say. Life, the best teacher of all, has usually led them to this awakening. I need only teach enough craft for them to put it down on the page, and create a safe environ to summon the muse. The aim is that *The Way of Story* workshops become a temple wherein attend oracles and angels.

Writing is not about being a writer, but about the experience of writing itself. I write in order to know myself. Through the inner journey of writing, I am better able to understand the world around me.

> What I represent every time I set out to achieve something is
> Myself.
> — Maya Angelou

If I learned one thing while working in Hollywood, it is this.
The powers that be rarely know what they are looking for or what
will guarantee commercial success.

> Don't listen to those who say, "It's not done that way." Michel-
> angelo would have painted the Sistine floor and it would surely
> be rubbed out by today.
> — Neil Simon

Studios pay marketing firms enormous funds to find what will
sell. One of these high-paying marketing firms once recommended
to a certain powerful studio to say no to two film projects: *E.T.* and
Star Wars. The lesson here is that it is always the original story that
touches a universal nerve in the general public, and wins the day.
Then what happens? The studios go about finding a lesser copy of
the original instead of searching for the next original story. There's
a saying in Hollywood: "We want something seen before — only a
little bit different." Go figure!

Creativity demands commitment and risk, and often mistakes
can be as important to the process of creativity as success. What
helps to get through the night is to see the whole not as product but as process — mistakes included. James Joyce once said,
"Mistakes are the portals of discovery." Also, it is always valuable
to know what you cannot do in order to focus on what you should
be doing.

> The man who has never made a mistake will never make
> anything.
> — George Bernard Shaw

In these uncertain economic times, I observe many who have
sacrificed their dream of writing for seeming security. They take
full-time jobs — only to lose them during an economic recession.
Great companies demanding loyalty and long hours now dismiss
thousands of workers daily. I cannot tell you how many individuals have come to *The Way of Story* workshops having lost their jobs

in Silicon Valley, or quit their jobs as speech writers in Washington D. C., or as advertising executives in order to return to their first dream: that of writing for and from themselves.

Don't play for safety. It's the most dangerous thing in the world.
— Hugh Walpole

Here's another example of playing it safe and losing. I read an article in the *Los Angeles Times* about Paramount Studios head Sherry Lansing, the first woman to head a major studio. The article is titled "Lansing seeks to pull Paramount out of a serious slump." To quote Rachel Abramowitz and John Horn: "Paramount's troubles can be seen as a parable of how an obsession with the bottom line in a creative business can ultimately backfire."

The article goes on to say that risk-aversion strategy also dimmed Paramount's creative vision. Interesting that one of their earlier successes was *Titanic*. Hollywood studios as well as other giant mega-corporations may sink when the basic roots of creativity and risk are neglected for the bottom line.

It is in the imagination that a man's highest values lie.
— C. G. Jung

That's the bottom line, not money. Ultimately, creativity matters — not career. Creativity matters not only for artistic product, but also for life — especially for life.

Once in New York, Violette Verdy, a prima ballerina for the New York City Ballet, introduced me to one of the great artists of our time, choreographer George Balanchine. Balanchine graciously allowed me to observe rehearsals. It was an extraordinary experience to silently watch this master creating a new ballet. The dancers were as pigments in his hand. He would become very still, stare blankly, then suddenly take an arm or a torso and shape it. Observing the sculptor Rodin at work would probably have been a similar experience.

Later Balanchine invited a few of us for supper at his apartment on the Upper West Side near Lincoln Center. There I watched the maestro cook in the same fashion in which he had choreographed. His concentration and delight was the same. Here was a creative life. Later after a sumptuous gourmet dinner, his cat performed for us. Yes, Balanchine had taught the cat to dance!

What struck me was that in Balanchine's mind, all of life was a creative experience. There was no separation between life and art. This is what I mean by advocating *The Way of Story* as a life path.

Any writer will tell you that there is no time when one is not discovering or developing stories. The trick is to remain open to what may come in.

For six years, J. K. Rowling worked at a number of jobs, saying "I proved to be the worst secretary ever." In meetings she would jot down story ideas instead of taking notes. She was fired from several jobs and quit others out of boredom. She drifted for a time. Then one day she was on her way to London when the train broke down for four hours. She was staring out the train window when the idea that would change her life came to her out of the blue. "I can't tell you why or what triggered it, " she stated in a *School Library Journal* interview, "but I saw Harry and the wizard school very plainly ... the idea of a boy who didn't know what he was." By the time her train reached London, Rowling had the basic story figured out for the first *Harry Potter* book! The rest is history.

Between acting jobs in New York, I once took a temp job as a typist for a medical research company. This was the first and last time I worked full-time in an office. After two weeks of typing graphs and figures, and slowly going bonkers, my boss discovered that the long list of columns of numbers didn't match. Consequently, the work of several days had to be discarded — as was I. Later that day, my agent arranged an audition for me for George C. Scott's production of Arthur Miller's *Death of a Salesman*. I said a quick prayer knowing that I wasn't equipped for anything else but to act, and prepared to meet the formidable Mr. Scott. You know what? I got the part.

> An artist is someone who can't do anything else.
> — Jasper Johns

One thing is certain: the creative, if it is strong, will sooner or later find its path. It is as inevitable as a small stream of water pushing through rock. Of course, it may take time, and there may be twists and turns along the way.

> Nearly every writer I know was going to be something else.
> — John Barth

In India, where I have spent many years, there is the belief that to follow *dharma,* the law of one's being, will guarantee the right path for the soul. It is said it's better to be a good servant if that is your dharma than a bad king. But — and here's the rub — you cannot commit halfway. One hundred percent faith in the process is required, and that is often challenged by the slings and arrows of Life. However, in the end, I am eternally grateful to that small inner voice which has said "no" to the world's clamor and "yes" to the way of soul.

Some believe that, life after life, the soul chooses what it needs on its continuous journey towards some final realization. If this is so, the outer details of our lives may be less important than the inner evolution of the Self. So much for an impressive resume! This said, however, I must stress that timing is all. Sometimes events occur that may have more to do with the future than the present. The following story is one example of this.

During my time as an actor in New York, I was introduced to Joseph Campbell, the mythologist. Unfortunately, though I enjoyed several social outings with Campbell and his wife, Jean, I was not ready for him. I lived and breathed theatre then; that was my world and I could not see beyond the stage. He gave me one of his books, which remained unread for years. Only later did I realize that Joseph Campbell was an oracle of what was to come. Only later would I appreciate his ground-breaking work in mythology when I returned to the graduate school where he left his papers: Pacifica Graduate Institute in Santa Barbara, where I currently teach part-time. Hear his splendid words as spoken on the PBS television series *The Power of Myth* interviews with Bill Moyers:

> Follow your bliss. There's something inside you that knows when you're in the center, which knows when you're on the beam or off the beam. And if you get off the beam to earn money, you've lost your life. And if you stay in the center and don't get any money, you still have your bliss.

Sometimes though, like Hansel and Gretel, you may lose your way in the woods of the world. Yet I have found that if the commitment to the inner way is strong, something will arise to pull you back to your authentic way. It may begin as a feeling that something is not quite right or, if you need a louder call, an illness or divorce or accident.

While visiting friends in Santa Fe, recovering from the heat stroke suffered in India, I was lying in a hammock, cloud gazing. Unexpectedly, the energy shifted, and everything seemed to brighten. I was held by something beyond my limited self, and I heard from a clear voice from within, the title for this book: *The Way of Story*. Then and there, as if summoned, I made a commitment to one day write a book with this title. However, it would be three more years before I actually sat down to write it. Often there may be a considerable lag between the vision and the manifestation. Look how long it took Moses to carry out his vision! I spent the next two years in graduate school studying depth psychology and mythology which provided confirmation of my own now recovered values plus invaluable tools to write not another play or movie, but a book instead.

To be a cultural creative today is to try and serve as a shaman, bridging the two worlds of spirit and form, inspiration and manifestation. It is essential now to bring all of your self to the writing table, and not just a fragmented mind and wounded heart. The soul of the world, *anima mundi,* is longing for such stories. It is as if the old gods, discontent with neglect, have spread their lure, calling out to writers who can listen from within. It is time for them to live again through you. It is time for the return of the feminine, as well, so needed to balance the outmoded paradigms of patriarchy. (Consider the overwhelming success of the novel, *The Da Vinci Code,* as one example of a writer who tapped into this collective need of the return of the feminine.) New myths are sorely needed. Myths are not half-truths but a deeper, *felt* truth.

Myths are roadmaps for how we live our lives.
— Joseph Campbell

Years ago, taking a break from working as a playwright in New York and teaching at The New School University, I applied and won a Fulbright Research Fellowship to study the actor-storyteller in India. I wanted to go to a place where theatre was more than mere entertainment, where story carried some deeper meaning. For a year, I studied still-existing Dravidian forms over five thousand years old: shamanic exorcism, dance-drama expressions of serpent, ancestor, and goddess worship. These pre-Hindu creative religious expressions bridged the worlds of life and art. It was a valuable year, yet entirely different from what I expected. I was called upon to unlearn everything I had been taught, to let go of my sense of separateness. Only then could I dissolve into a multi-layered culture like India. I learned how, as a Westerner, I had been educated away from any sense of connectedness. I learned how I — and those like me — would stand apart, alienated yet full of hubris, and wonder why we were not whole and happy. There had to be a way back to Self, and for me, the way was story.

Myth [*story*] is how we make sense in a senseless world.
    — Rollo May

A few years later, I would write an episode for *Touched by an Angel* about an eight-year-old girl who was still connected to the Divine, who heard angel voices. Of course nobody believed her, and many were made uncomfortable by her light. The opening scene is on the playground where the little girl is being taunted for being different, while the angels observe the scene. The younger angel asks her mentor, played by Della Reese, "Tess, when human beings are born knowing who they are, how is it that they forget?" Tess replies, "They call it education."

This line was cut from the show when it aired. When I asked our producer why, she said, "Because it might offend teachers." Know that you take a risk when you challenge the system.

Once I was present during a panel of filmmakers from East Berlin and Hollywood. This was before the Berlin Wall fell. What struck me was the East Berliner commenting on how even in Hollywood, there is repression and censorship. The only difference here is that the writer censors himself, lest it not be commercial enough. Good point!

Surely, it is time to create new myths that will better serve the soul.

A civilization needs a myth in order to live.
— Marie-Louise von Franz

Story can answer the deep human need to find meaning, and, consequently, provide hope. Story can teach tolerance, a quality needed more today than ever. By evoking our ability to care what happens to someone else, story nourishes compassion. Of course, story can do the reverse, as well — as shown in any local movie theatre. Here, I am referring to stories which nourish soul.

How often have our young people spoken of being lost, not being one's self, or being split off? How many victims of trauma have spoken of feeling disconnected from the body at the moment of trauma? Is this so far removed from the shaman's perspective? Perhaps we should look back, pre-Freud, to the simple shaman's role and its ancient wisdom. What constitutes this wisdom of the past then? Shamanic training often involves learning rituals, songs, and chants to aid in the process of healing. In her remarkable book, *Shaman*, Joan Halifax writes:

> The shaman as artist and performer utilizes the imagination to give form to a cosmos that is unpredictable... Order is imposed on chaos; form is given to psychic confusion; the journey finds its direction... And it is the transition to this verbal expression... which induces the release of the physiological process.

Story carries a special power in the lives of young people. Far better to allow youth a safe container for their dark side rather than to have them self-destruct or commit some crime. The trick is to offer them a safe and appropriate outlet.

I witnessed a transforming effect over and over again when I was asked by the Dramatist Guild to help launch the Young Playwrights Program in the New York City public schools. I joined such playwrights as Tony Award–winning playwright Terrence McNally, and ventured out into the junior high and high schools, teaching playwriting. After several classes, we would encourage the students to write a one-act play and enter it into the annual competition, the

Young Playwrights Festival. The winners, ages 8-19, would have a professional off-Broadway production in New York and Avon Publishers would publish their plays. This ambitious project gave value to creative writing, and the results were absolutely amazing. Full productions were mounted at Joseph Papp's Public Theatre or at Playwrights Horizons enabling the young writers to see their plays come alive. One writer was all of eight years old!

> Theatre glamorizes thought and reveals the human heart. This makes it as important as the scientist, psychologist, or minister.
> — Lawrence Olivier

How to convince government today that cultivating the arts is essential for a balanced society? Creativity is not simply for artists. Whether one becomes a professional creative or not is beside the point. The arts are necessary in order to develop the heart. And without heart, we are in danger. "The world hangs on a slender thread," Jung wrote, "and that is the psyche of man."

> Art establishes the basic human truths which must serve as the touchstones of our judgment. The artist, however faithful to his vision of reality, becomes the last champion of the individual mind and sensibility against an intrusive society.
> — John F. Kennedy

What world do we wish to live in today? What are the models we will offer to our children? As a writer, what world will you create?

> I have made my world and it is a much better world than I ever saw outside.
> — Louise Nevelson, sculptor

Clearly, we cannot begin to create a new world without taking risks. In my own life, I have followed the way of risk by being a freelance everything: actor, playwright, screenwriter, teacher, and author. Though tempted, I have turned down tenure-track university positions, staff writing for one-hour television series, and other lucrative jobs, preferring part-time writing assignments and adjunct teaching. Not everyone should travel the outlying paths, but I knew it was my way. For some reason, I would change careers about every ten years: acting, playwriting, and teaching. Family and friends were often concerned as I would leave work and spend months in India meditating or walking the coasts of Cornwall. Yet in the long run, it pays off. It is not a career move but rather a soul move.

Of course, I will not deny that sometimes there may be a price for choosing the way of risk. But isn't there a price to pay whatever you choose? I have found that to follow the way of soul is always the sure path, in every sense — even financial, in the end. The process takes one deeper into the recesses of Self, and from there, boundless treasures emerge.

If, in embracing the way of change, we fear losing our "identity," we have only to reflect on how many different roles we already play in life. Daughter, professional woman, wife, or ex-wife; son, father, employer, lover — we are many things to many people. I sometimes think of the various hats we wear as images on a cinema screen. Costumes and stories, even the players are forever changing, yet the Background or Self remains the same. The screen is not the stories projected upon it any more than we are what we do. It is the screen or rather the Self that interests me more and more. This changeless Background is what is essential.

The *Way of Story* is a life path. Long-term vision is what is required, and a deep commitment for the journey. The interesting part is that following the inner *way of story,* which I advocate throughout this book, is ultimately the most practical course, in every sense. Follow your soul. Dare to mark your individual path, for now and ever before, the authentic voice is the final solution.

For those committed to an inner journey, meditation is not just sitting in the corner with closed eyes. The whole of life can be a meditation. If this is so, writing, too, can be a meditative act. It depends entirely on the approach or intention. For those who adopt the perspective of writing for the Soul, writing will be a spiritual journey, enriching every aspect of the life.

Here, ritual can be useful. I created an altar in my writing room, with candle, sacred photographs, and a crystal or precious stones. Each morning, I light the candle and do a brief meditation before settling down to write. It shapes the day and the work, providing a sense of higher purpose and meaning. It makes me feel good in that I am connecting with something greater than myself.

Life's journey is a movement towards wholeness. Hold fast to your dreams, your myths, and your stories — both personal and collective. May they become a clear beacon on your soul's journey. This, after all, is nothing less than life's purpose.

From Rumi, the thirteenth-century Persian mystic and poet, I leave you with the following invocation (translated by Coleman Barks):

> Try and be a sheet of paper with nothing on it.
> Be a spot of ground where nothing is growing,
> Where something might be planted,
> a seed, possibly, from the Absolute.
> Stop the words now.
> Open the window in the center of your chest,
> and let the spirits fly in and out.

Chapter 12

A Guide to The Way of Story Workshops

I've got something in me, I don't know what, that wants to
soar.
— Rimbaud

RECENTLY, I WAS invited to present an exploration into creativity at a conference in Spain. I guided the participants — scientists, doctors, businessmen, psychiatrists, teachers, writers — through some of the exercises in *The Way of Story* book. A few weeks later, a woman from California, who had attended the conference, invited me to lunch. She wanted to share with me her experience of doing the exercises and hearing me talk. A published writer herself, she said something profound had happened to her because of that day. "I don't remember what you said, but here's what came through as I wrote." Then again, she commented, "I don't remember the exercise but here's what gushed out." And so on. I sat there, smiling, then said, "You've confirmed exactly what I had hoped would happen." I then went on to share that my aim was not to have her remember me or what I had said, but to have a transcendent experience of writing from the depth, a pouring forth — which is precisely what had happened to her in Spain.

Here was a published author in her late sixties, and yet the workshop became a catalyst, mining areas heretofore untapped. A retired psychiatrist once took the workshop, and shared that he came to keep his brain cells alive and alert. He was ninety-two, and delighted us all. Some return again and again, saying the workshop serves as a jump start to get them writing again. My philosophy of being a teacher is simply to become a catalyst for others to discover themselves and free their own potential, to create the space where magic happens. So the intention is to free the story, fulfilling not my vision, but theirs.

The Way of Story book is now being used in several writing programs at universities such as New York University as well as various high schools. I have also heard from readers here and there who have started writing groups to continue the Way of Story. Though I continue to travel and teach the workshops both in the States, Europe, and Asia, I thought it might be a good idea to include a chapter with some suggestions and descriptions on leading the workshops. So, here is my approach, yet feel free to find your own, along the way. Remember there are many roads to Rome!

The workshop — as the book — is for all forms of narrative writing, including memoir, novel, biography, plays, screenplays, narrative poetry or songs. It is for both professionals (who seek to recover the freshness they began with) and beginning writers (who, though enthusiastic, seek craft). These two groups have much to learn from one another. It is vital to create a safe and sacred space in which to respect the creative process, leaving judgment or competitive urges behind. This is a lab — not a final performance with finished products.

Attendance is limited to 20 or 30 participants to provide sufficient one on one feedback. (I also speak at large conferences using the same material in the book though there is less opportunity for individual feedback.)

All that is needed is a white board or flip paper chart with markers. Also useful is a CD player with a selected CD of relaxing instrumental music such as gentle flute, nature sounds, etc. Each participant will need paper and pen — some may wish to use a laptop. Here are some ideas as to how to lead the workshop. Take what is useful and add your own touch to it as well.

When possible, I seat everyone in a wide circle, as used in sacred initiations, so as to dispel any classroom association. If the workshop is two days long, this usually means 9 a.m. to 4 p.m. with a one-hour break for lunch. (Best to have the group stay and eat together, as it helps everyone to bond.)

I pepper a lot of quotes throughout the book which can be useful if teaching a semester or year-long class in high school or university. My students quickly learn to first look on the board for a new quote about creativity, and are invited to share some of their personal favorites. On the black or white board, I write the first quote found in the first chapter: "The world is made up of stories, not atoms" (Muriel Rukeyser).

On the second day, I usually write one of my own quotes: "Sitting down is the hardest part."

Sometimes I am asked to teach a five-day intensive, as at the Esalen Institute, which provides more time to explore and share. I assign assignment exercises at night to bring in the next day to share and receive feedback, as well as use improvisations in which participants can learn to write spontaneously from feelings and physical sensation. Often I am asked to do a one-day version of the workshop and have even presented a three-hour version. Best, however, is to do at least a two-day workshop. When I teach at universities, of course, I create a syllabus for either one semester or two semesters. There is ample material in the book to provide for this, as well.

When asked what participants need to take the workshop, I usually say, "Two things: writing materials and courage." For this workshop is not only about learning craft, but about having the courage to open and plumb your very depths. Writing can be a spiritual journey once you allow your wings to spread.

> My teacher told me one thing. Live in the soul.
> — Lalla, female Sufi

I encourage all ages from twelve years on. Once on Orcas Island, Washington, I had a group of twenty-eight participants: the youngest was twelve, the eldest was eighty-four. The group dynamic was splendid, and the twelve-year-old turned out to be one of the best writers! I personally think we segregate too readily, for there is so much to learn from mixing disciplines, genders, and ages. One of the joys of leading the workshops is seeing how each one is unique, depending upon the individual participants. In fact, I tend to adapt the approach and choice of exercises to the group at hand. For instance, if more are interested in writing a certain genre, i.e., screenwriting or memoir, then I spend more time there. If there are those more intuitive or spiritually oriented, this will also change the dynamic and approach. One man from Utah wrote saying, *"The Way of Story* was a spiritual experience, as well as practical."

Day One

The group has gathered for Day One of a two-day Way of Story workshop. They are seated in a circle and have pen and paper, and a copy of *The Way of Story* book which they may or may not have already read. I do a greeting and orientation informing them that this approach is for both the right and left side of the brain. They are invited to bring all of themselves to the process. It is a voyage of discovery. For those who know what story they wish to focus on, I suggest they gear each of the exercises to their chosen story. For those who have yet to find their story, I tell them that usually by simply doing each exercise, they will discover their story — or their story will find them. I encourage them to see the group as a resource. Once I had a writer who was doing a project on nuclear energy and another man in the group happened to run a nuclear power plant! So guess who sat next to each other at lunchtime?

I share a bit about my own journey as a writer and teacher, and how I came to this holistic approach to writing. Then I ask each participant to introduce themselves, what they do for a living, where they live, what writing experience they have had, what genre interests them, and, most importantly, what they hope to gain from the workshop.

This done, they are asked to set down their pen and paper, and close their eyes for the visualization. First, I play the CD softly, read the Prologue which begins, "In the beginning was Story...," then proceed to guide them through the Soul Dialogue visualization found at the end of Chapter 1. After this inner journey, I invite them to take up their pen and write for ten minutes. The purpose of this activity is to ask that deeper part of ourselves, the Soul, what it wants of us. This is for each participant and is not to be shared openly with the group. It simply serves to open the portal and invite the Muse to play.

How to choose your story opens a short talk on where stories come from (see Chapter 1: In the Beginning Was Story). The key is to suggest they choose the story they feel the greatest connection with, for it is the power of emotional connection that proves contagious to both reader and audience. Encourage them to write from themselves, let their intuition guide, and open so that the spirits may have their way with them.

Next, I generally speak about Character and my preference for character-driven stories. Time for the first character exercise, found near the beginning of Chapter 5. Pick a real-life character from your own experience, one who most influenced you before the age of 21 or so. There is a list of questions to ask which can be helpful in the same chapter. I stress that it must be someone known personally — not Lawrence of Arabia or Luke Skywalker. Allow ten minutes to write, then ask those who wish to share with the group. Urge them to find a visual metaphor to symbolize the character, often a parent, teacher, or grandparent. The sharing will invite comments from me, and then become open for others to provide feedback. (Stress the importance of constructive feedback.)

By now, it is probably time for a lunch break. I usually have lunch catered so we can stay together. I suggest breaking only for an hour. My one rule is not to talk directly about what we talk about in class, but to get to know each other. Quite quickly, it is time to return to work or play, if you will.

The afternoon session begins with a solid, academic focus on the craft of writing: Seven Steps to Story Structure (Chapter 2). I write all the steps on the white board, then return and go through them a second time, this time using an example provided in the chapter. It may be useful to repeat this process by choosing a film or book known to most or all, and apply the seven steps more than once. Important to have this under your belt, as it is a lifelong tool for writing, and serves all forms of narrative.

Time for the next exercise found at the end of Chapter 4: Tracking Story Specifics: The Secret to Successful Rewrites. Write in two sentences what your story is about. It works best if the first sentence tells what the story is about, introducing a main character, and the second reveals the theme or purpose of your story. It may be useful to provide several examples of Hollywood log lines, also found in Chapter 4. Important to let the participants know that though this is the shortest of all the exercises, it is generally the most challenging. Allow ten minutes for writing. When sharing, invite feedback from all. This back and forth becomes a replica to a story development meeting in Hollywood. There is something about talking out loud which can stimulate and help discover the right way to use the words.

Instead of taking an afternoon tea break, I generally suggest a silent walk exercise. Participants are to leave writing materials behind, and simply and silently walk alone, observing all they see, allowing the impressions to tap memory associations and feelings. They might also look for sensory detail useful for the portrayal of their characters. It can also be a search for metaphor: for that animal, bird, stone, or flower which symbolizes their character or theme, and why. Upon returning, allow ten minutes for writing, incorporating at least one incident or object observed or some useful detail glimpsed which serves as a metaphor for their story, theme, or character. The sharing is a reminder to use our senses when we write as well as that golden chest of memories, and also to write not only from the left, logical brain.

If time is short, simply write on the board and explain three short exercises due the next day. Also some may wish to rewrite their two-sentence story exercise done earlier and bring it in for feedback.

The homework exercises are the following (found in Chapter 6: The Secret of Writing Stunning Dialogue):

- Eavesdropping Dialogue Exercise
- 2+1 Dialogue Exercise
- Emotional Monologue Exercise

Choose a main character in your story and write a first-person monologue. Let there be another person in the room with him, to whom he is speaking. Now let the situation be such that it brings out an extreme emotion from your speaking character: joy, despair, fear, anger, etc. Write one page of monologue in the first person from the character's point of view. The goal of this exercise is not to provide exposition as to plot but to push your character towards an extreme feeling. It need not make sense, just go with it. What matters here is to *feel* the emotion, then to write whatever comes. Again, write whatever arises from the extreme feeling chosen.

If there is still time before concluding the first day, allow a few minutes of writing time to get them started on the homework exercises listed above. Writing silently in a group can be the encouragement needed to prime the pump.

DAY TWO

Invite a brief check-in of each individual's process thus far. Any blocks? Why? Some of the exercises may seem easier, others difficult; some writers may still be struggling with telling their story in two sentences, and so on. Some may have had a breakthrough, or help from a dream during the night. At least one or two may have discovered which story they wish to write, if they didn't know before. By now, many have shared and are sitting in the wide, safe circle, eager to begin Day Two.

For a fun warm up, I lead them in an oral round robin group exercise. I tell them that the story need not be logical or make any sense at all, and encourage them to be specific, to add characters and story twists. I begin a story in two or three sentences then say, "And then..." and the next person takes it up building a story in a few sentences. Then each says "And then..." and it passes to the person sitting to their right. The last person has the challenge of ending the story. Much laughter later, at the end of the round robin story, there is spontaneous applause. Then I remind that you can write as children play, with all the freshness and mysterious wonder of what will happen next, simply by taking the plunge with your imaginations. (Sometimes I start with the round robin storytelling and only afterwards, they will share what is going on with their process. To decide the order, I simply allow my intuition to guide me with each individual group.)

It is time to share what has been written, beginning with the Eavesdropping Dialogue Exercise. I invite each writer to cast the other character and read together. This is not only more fun, but important to hear the separate voices of their character's dialogue. It is also fun to have the class later try and guess the line over-heard. Sometimes, I get them on their feet and do an improvisation based on the same premise, making up the lines as they go along. They and the class are often amazed at how much better —more real — the spoken lines are than what had been written down. Dialogue is not conversation (see Chapter 6: The Secret of Writing Stunning Dialogue).

After several shares, I will do a mini-lecture on finding your voice as a writer, and also finding your character's voice by discovering their perspective or POV (see Chapter 9: The Voice of the Story). It usually makes a strong impression to share the true story of the little boy asked to give his blood to save his sister's life. I also mention that making your story character-driven will add more power to the message you are trying to get across (Chapter 5: Creating Character-Driven Stories).

Next we open the stage to share the Emotional Monologue Exercise (Chapter 6: The Secret of Writing Stunning Dialogue) which participants did as homework. The purpose of this exercise is to write from an extreme feeling; the exposition of the scene is less important. Here, again, improvisations can be useful. To site one example from an earlier Way of Story workshop:

One woman had quite a brilliant mind but when she read her monologue to the rest of the class, it was dry and did not ring true. Same as when she did a dialogue exercise. Why? She had written it entirely from her rational brain. I told her to put her paper down and to stand up with another randomly selected student. Then I asked them to stand facing one another with the palms of both their hands touching, so that they were forming a bridge. I asked them to push as hard as they could as if trying to force the other person to back up. After a moment of this, I told her to keep pushing with her hands and at the same time to start improvising a monologue — not what she had written but as if she were the character in that situation and it was occurring to her at this very moment. Now. The difference was night and day. Everyone applauded and said this was so much more effective, moving, and real. Then occurred the moment every teacher waits for: the light bulb went off in her head, and she smiled this great smile, letting me know that she understood. Sometimes in teaching, too, you learn more by doing than talking about it! She had learned organically with her whole body and emotions that she must write in the same manner — that is to say, with her whole self. It is not enough to write with one part of your brain. Equally valuable tools are a writer's emotions, memories, intuition, guts. It is so important to bring all of you to the table.

Another memorable example is from a more intensive five-day workshop given at the Esalen Institute. An older gentleman had wanted for years to write a memoir of his experience in World War II. He was in the first group of American soldiers liberating a concentration camp in Poland. He first read the monologue which had little or no emotion in it, and seemed a distant accounting of what he had seen. I asked him to submit to an experiment using improvisation. He was game. I had six of the other participants lie down on the floor in varying positions. Then I had the former soldier sit on a chair in the middle of the room. First I had him close his eyes and lead him in a visualization to take him back to the exact moment when he entered the camp. I told him that it was not many years ago, but today, this very moment. When you open your eyes, I want you to look at the bodies on the floor and tell me what you see and how you feel about what you see. A few moments after he opened his eyes, he stared at one of the men lying on the floor and came over, kneeling down to him. Then he began to weep, and returned to the chair. Then he began to tell us the story, a story he had blocked from his memory. He shared that he had found a man on the ground, believed dead, but was still alive. He was so thin, emaciated that he couldn't at first believe he was still breathing, but he was. Well, every participant in that room soon had tears in their eyes, though none had responded to what he had written earlier. At the break, the old soldier came up to me, took my hand in both of his, and said, "Thank you. Thank you. Now I know why I had to wait so long to write this story. I had to feel the memory."

The second day of the workshop is devoted mostly to the sharing and feedback of what has come as a result of the exercises. If the workshop is longer than two days, more exercises are done, and more topics covered. If it is an ongoing class or writers group, spend sufficient time on developing a story outline (see Chapter 3: Writing the Story Outline). The longer the writer works and reworks the outline, the more time is saved when settling in to write the book or screenplay. This is the blueprint and, though not written in stone, will offer the underlying structure of the story.

When I speak at conferences to a large audience, I use an overhead projector with laminated pages to be projected (Power Point works well, too). Most often, the topics covered are the Seven Steps to Story Structure, Story Outline example, and a chart of the number of pages in each act for varying formats (feature, teleplay, or 1-hour series).

If time permits, the Personal Myth exercise is a good one to do towards the end of the workshop (see Chapter 9: The Voice of the Story). First have class members write a personal myth or fairytale they have always loved. Allow five or ten minutes for this. Then have them write their own personal myth based on the fairy tale or myth they have just written. This is an excellent way to make the story your own. If time allows, these can be read and discussed within the group. Quite often they are surprised which myth pops up, and only when they complete the second part of the exercise do they realize why this myth or story chose them. It is a voyage of self-discovery, and a realization of what it is they want to write about. Once I was presenting the workshop in England, and a man in his late thirties was puzzled why he chose *Robinson Crusoe* for his myth. This produced a kind of epiphany, bringing him back into touch with his core values and sense of adventure. This realization became a guide in choosing which stories to write. He was one of those who later shared that the workshop had been more than a writing class. It had been, for him, life-changing.

Day Two is coming to a close; hopefully all who wish to share have had the opportunity to do so. I leave at least ten minutes for Q and A, so that the class is free to ask whatever they wish. To close, the visualization at the end of Chapter 1 is repeated, only this time instead of asking Soul what it wants, each will write a response or commitment to Soul. It might be a commitment to spend two hours daily writing or to complete a project begun earlier, or whatever arises for each participant. These are private and will not be shared.

There are many more exercises than described in this chapter, so best to flip through the book and review the Exercises **indented** so easy to spot. Find the ones best suited to your group's needs. It is also a good idea to have everyone list their name, address, and email, then make copies and hand out on Day Two. Sometimes *Way of Story* writing groups are formed this way, continuing the process and providing support.

Many who have experienced *The Way of Story* workshops have shared later that it was, for them, life-changing, a spiritual as well as practical experience. Perhaps this is because a safe and sacred space is provided as well as carefully designed exercises for the sole purpose of writing from within. In this way, whatever story emerges is unique.

CREATING NETWORKS & RESOURCES

> Writers must stick together like beggars and thieves.
> — Ernest Hemingway

As I travel about America (and now the world) teaching *The Way of Story* workshops, I encourage participants to create writing groups in their area, meeting once a week or month. This generates deadlines and an audience for feedback on what you've written. Writing is a solitary affair, and support groups can be a creative catalyst and professional network, as well as creatively and psychologically nurturing. Also, there is something about committing to writing that makes things happen.

What matters is to summon the courage and the heart, and write — or teach — from within. Now, all that is needed is to take the plunge, entering the way of story.

> Whatever you can do, or dream you can, begin it. Boldness has genius, power and magic in it. Begin it now.
> — Goethe

About the Author

*C*ATHERINE ANN JONES has played major roles in over fifty productions on and off Broadway, as well as television (*Great Performances*, etc.) and film. Disappointed by the lack of good roles for women, she wrote a play about Virginia Woolf (*On the Edge*) which won a National Endowment for the Arts Award. Ten of her plays, including *Calamity Jane* (both play and musical) and *The Women of Cedar Creek*, have won several awards and are produced both in and out of New York. Her films include *The Christmas Wife* (Jason Robards & Julie Harris), *Unlikely Angel* (Dolly Parton), *Angel Passing* (Hume Cronyn & Teresa Wright), which played at Sundance and went on to garner fifteen awards here and abroad, and the popular TV series, *Touched by an Angel*. A Fulbright Scholar to India, she has taught writing at The New School University, University of Southern California, Pacifica Graduate Institute, and the Esalen Institute. Ms. Jones lives in Ojai, California, and leads The Way of Story workshops throughout the United States, Europe, and Asia. For her workshop schedule, blog, and story/script consultant service please visit *www.wayofstory.com*.

"We've become lopsided living only in our heads. Writing, in order to serve the soul, must integrate outer craft with the inner world of intuition and feeling."
— Catherine Ann Jones, quoted in the *New York Times*

THE WRITER'S JOURNEY
3RD EDITION

MYTHIC STRUCTURE FOR WRITERS

CHRISTOPHER VOGLER

BEST SELLER
OVER 170,000 COPIES SOLD!

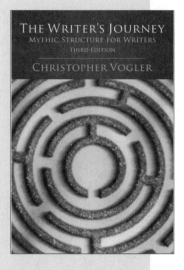

See why this book has become an international best seller and a true classic. *The Writer's Journey* explores the powerful relationship between mythology and storytelling in a clear, concise style that's made it required reading for movie executives, screenwriters, playwrights, scholars, and fans of pop culture all over the world.

Both fiction and nonfiction writers will discover a set of useful myth-inspired storytelling paradigms (i.e., "The Hero's Journey") and step-by-step guidelines to plot and character development. Based on the work of Joseph Campbell, *The Writer's Journey* is a must for all writers interested in further developing their craft.

The updated and revised third edition provides new insights and observations from Vogler's ongoing work on mythology's influence on stories, movies, and man himself.

"This book is like having the smartest person in the story meeting come home with you and whisper what to do in your ear as you write a screenplay. Insight for insight, step for step, Chris Vogler takes us through the process of connecting theme to story and making a script come alive."
> – Lynda Obst, Producer, *Sleepless in Seattle, How to Lose a Guy in 10 Days;*
> Author, *Hello, He Lied*

"This is a book about the stories we write, and perhaps more importantly, the stories we live. It is the most influential work I have yet encountered on the art, nature, and the very purpose of storytelling."
> – Bruce Joel Rubin, Screenwriter, *Stuart Little 2, Deep Impact,*
> *Ghost, Jacob's Ladder*

CHRISTOPHER VOGLER is a veteran story consultant for major Hollywood film companies and a respected teacher of filmmakers and writers around the globe. He has influenced the stories of movies from *The Lion King* to *Fight Club* to *The Thin Red Line* and most recently wrote the first installment of *Ravenskull*, a Japanese-style manga or graphic novel. He is the executive producer of the feature film *P.S. Your Cat is Dead* and writer of the animated feature *Jester Till*.

$26.95 · 300 PAGES · ORDER NUMBER 76RLS · ISBN: 193290736x

SAVE THE CAT! GOES TO THE MOVIES

THE SCREENWRITER'S GUIDE TO EVERY STORY EVER TOLD

BLAKE SNYDER

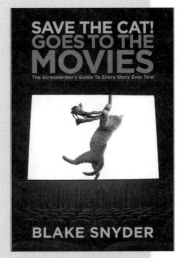

In the long-awaited sequel to his surprise bestseller, *Save the Cat!*, author and screenwriter Blake Snyder returns to form in a fast-paced follow-up that proves why his is the most talked-about approach to screenwriting in years. In the perfect companion piece to his first book, Snyder delivers even more insider's information gleaned from a 20-year track record as "one of Hollywood's most successful spec screenwriters," giving you the clues to write *your* movie.

Designed for screenwriters, novelists, and movie fans, this book gives readers the key breakdowns of the 50 most instructional movies from the past 30 years. From *M*A*S*H* to *Crash*, from *Alien* to *Saw*, from *10* to *Eternal Sunshine of the Spotless Mind*, Snyder reveals how screenwriters who came before you tackled the same challenges you are facing with the film you want to write — or the one you are currently working on.

Writing a "rom-com"? Check out the "Buddy Love" chapter for a "beat for beat" dissection of *When Harry Met Sally...* plus references to 10 other great romantic comedies that will make your story sing.

Want to execute a great mystery? Go to the "Whydunit" section and learn about the "dark turn" that's essential to the heroes of *All the President's Men*, *Blade Runner*, *Fargo* and hip noir *Brick* — and see why ALL good stories, whether a Hollywood blockbuster or a Sundance award winner, follow the same rules of structure outlined in Snyder's breakthrough method.

If you want to sell your script and create a movie that pleases most audiences most of the time, the odds increase if you reference Snyder's checklists and see what makes 50 films tick. After all, both executives and audiences respond to the same elements good writers seek to master. They want to know the type of story they signed on for, and whether it's structured in a way that satisfies everyone. It's what they're looking for. And now, it's what you can deliver.

BLAKE SNYDER, besides selling million-dollar scripts to both Disney and Spielberg, is still "one of Hollywood's most successful spec screenwriters," having made another spec sale in 2006. An in-demand scriptcoach and seminar and workshop leader, Snyder provides information for writers through his website, *www.blakesnyder.com*.

$24.95 · 270 PAGES · ORDER NUMBER 75RLS · ISBN: 1932907351

MYTH AND THE MOVIES

DISCOVERING THE MYTHIC STRUCTURE OF 50 UNFORGETTABLE FILMS

STUART VOYTILLA

FOREWORD BY CHRISTOPHER VOGLER
AUTHOR OF *THE WRITER'S JOURNEY*

BEST SELLER
OVER 20,000 COPIES SOLD!

An illuminating companion piece to *The Writer's Journey*, *Myth and the Movies* applies the mythic structure Vogler developed to 50 well-loved U.S. and foreign films. This comprehensive book offers a greater understanding of why some films continue to touch and connect with audiences generation after generation.

Movies discussed include *The Godfather*, *Some Like It Hot*, *Citizen Kane*, *Halloween*, *Jaws*, *Annie Hall*, *Chinatown*, *The Fugitive*, *Sleepless in Seattle*, *The Graduate*, *Dances with Wolves*, *Beauty and the Beast*, *Platoon*, and *Die Hard*.

"Stuart Voytilla's Myth and the Movies *is a remarkable achievement: an ambitious, thought-provoking, and cogent analysis of the mythic underpinnings of fifty great movies. It should prove a valuable resource for film teachers, students, critics, and especially screenwriters themselves, whose challenge, as Voytilla so clearly understands, is to constantly reinvent a mythology for our times."*
> – Ted Tally, Academy Award® Screenwriter, *Silence of the Lambs*

"Myth and the Movies is a must for every writer who wants to tell better stories. Voytilla guides his readers to a richer and deeper understanding not only of mythic structure, but also of the movies we love."*
> – Christopher Wehner, Web editor
> *The Screenwriters Utopia* and *Creative Screenwriting*

"I've script consulted for ten years and I've studied every genre thoroughly. I thought I knew all their nuances – until I read Voytilla's book. This ones goes on my Recommended Reading List. A fascinating analysis of the Hero's Myth for all genres."
> – Lou Grantt, *Hollywood Scriptwriter* Magazine

STUART VOYTILLA is a screenwriter, literary consultant, teacher, and author of *Writing the Comedy Film*.

$26.95 · 300 PAGES · ORDER NUMBER 39RLS · ISBN: 0941188663

24 HOURS | 1.800.833.5738 | WWW.MWP.COM

MICHAEL WIESE PRODUCTIONS

Since 1981, Michael Wiese Productions has been dedicated to providing both novice and seasoned filmmakers with vital information on all aspects of filmmaking. We have published nearly 100 books, used in over 600 film schools and countless universities, and by hundreds of thousands of filmmakers worldwide.

Our authors are successful industry professionals who spend innumerable hours writing about the hard stuff: budgeting, financing, directing, marketing, and distribution. They believe that if they share their knowledge and experience with others, more high quality films will be produced.

And that has been our mission, now complemented through our new web-based resources. We invite all readers to visit www.mwp.com to receive free tipsheets and sample chapters, participate in forum discussions, obtain product discounts — and even get the opportunity to receive free books, project consulting, and other services offered by our company.

Our goal is, quite simply, to help you reach your goals. That's why we give our readers the most complete portal for filmmaking knowledge available — in the most convenient manner.

We truly hope that our books and web-based resources will empower you to create enduring films that will last for generations to come.

Let us hear from you at anytime.

Sincerely,
Michael Wiese
Publisher, Filmmaker

www.mwp.com

FILM & VIDEO BOOKS

Cinematic Storytelling: *The 100 Most Powerful Film Conventions Every Filmmaker Must Know* / Jennifer Van Sijll / $24.95

Complete DVD Book, The: *Designing, Producing, and Marketing Your Independent Film on DVD* / Chris Gore and Paul J. Salamoff / $26.95

Complete Independent Movie Marketing Handbook, The: *Promote, Distribute & Sell Your Film or Video* / Mark Steven Bosko / $39.95

Could It Be a Movie?: *How to Get Your Ideas Out of Your Head and Up on the Screen* / Christina Hamlett / $26.95

Creating Characters: *Let Them Whisper Their Secrets* Marisa D'Vari / $26.95

Crime Writer's Reference Guide, The: *1001 Tips for Writing the Perfect Crime* Martin Roth / $20.95

Cut by Cut: *Editing Your Film or Video* Gael Chandler / $35.95

Digital Filmmaking 101, 2nd Edition: *An Essential Guide to Producing Low-Budget Movies* / Dale Newton and John Gaspard / $26.95

Digital Moviemaking, 2nd Edition: *All the Skills, Techniques, and Moxie You'll Need to Turn Your Passion into a Career* / Scott Billups / $26.95

Directing Actors: *Creating Memorable Performances for Film and Television* Judith Weston / $26.95

Directing Feature Films: *The Creative Collaboration Between Directors, Writers, and Actors* / Mark Travis / $26.95

Eye is Quicker, The: *Film Editing; Making a Good Film Better* Richard D. Pepperman / $27.95

Fast, Cheap & Under Control: *Lessons Learned from the Greatest Low-Budget Movies of All Time* / John Gaspard / $26.95

Film & Video Budgets, 4th Updated Edition Deke Simon and Michael Wiese / $26.95

Film Directing: Cinematic Motion, 2nd Edition Steven D. Katz / $27.95

Film Directing: Shot by Shot, *Visualizing from Concept to Screen* Steven D. Katz / $27.95

Film Director's Intuition, The: *Script Analysis and Rehearsal Techniques* Judith Weston / $26.95

Film Production Management 101: *The Ultimate Guide for Film and Television Production Management and Coordination* / Deborah S. Patz / $39.95

Filmmaking for Teens: *Pulling Off Your Shorts* Troy Lanier and Clay Nichols / $18.95

First Time Director: *How to Make Your Breakthrough Movie* Gil Bettman / $27.95

From Word to Image: *Storyboarding and the Filmmaking Process* Marcie Begleiter / $26.95

Hitting Your Mark, 2nd Edition: *Making a Life – and a Living – as a Film Director* Steve Carlson / $22.95

Hollywood Standard, The: *The Complete and Authoritative Guide to Script Format and Style* / Christopher Riley / $18.95

I Could've Written a Better Movie Than That!: *How to Make Six Figures as a Script Consultant even if You're not a Screenwriter* / Derek Rydall / $26.95

Independent Film Distribution: *How to Make a Successful End Run Around the Big Guys* / Phil Hall / $24.95

Independent Film and Videomakers Guide – 2nd Edition, The: *Expanded and Updated* / Michael Wiese / $29.95

Inner Drives: *How to Write and Create Characters Using the Eight Classic Centers of Motivation* / Pamela Jaye Smith / $26.95

I'll Be in My Trailer!: *The Creative Wars Between Directors & Actors* John Badham and Craig Modderno / $26.95

Moral Premise, The: *Harnessing Virtue & Vice for Box Office Success* Stanley D. Williams, Ph.D. / $24.95

Myth and the Movies: *Discovering the Mythic Structure of 50 Unforgettable Films* / Stuart Voytilla / $26.95

On the Edge of a Dream: *Magic and Madness in Bali* Michael Wiese / $16.95

Perfect Pitch, The: *How to Sell Yourself and Your Movie Idea to Hollywood* Ken Rotcop / $16.95

Power of Film, The Howard Suber / $27.95

Psychology for Screenwriters: *Building Conflict in your Script* William Indick, Ph.D. / $26.95

Save the Cat!: *The Last Book on Screenwriting You'll Ever Need* Blake Snyder / $19.95

Screenwriting 101: *The Essential Craft of Feature Film Writing* Neill D. Hicks / $16.95

Screenwriting for Teens: *The 100 Principles of Screenwriting Every Budding Writer Must Know* / Christina Hamlett / $18.95

Script-Selling Game, The: *A Hollywood Insider's Look at Getting Your Script Sold and Produced* / Kathie Fong Yoneda / $16.95

Selling Your Story in 60 Seconds: *The Guaranteed Way to get Your Screenplay or Novel Read* / Michael Hauge / $12.95

Setting Up Your Scenes: *The Inner Workings of Great Films* Richard D. Pepperman / $24.95

Setting Up Your Shots: *Great Camera Moves Every Filmmaker Should Know* Jeremy Vineyard / $19.95

Shaking the Money Tree, 2nd Edition: *The Art of Getting Grants and Donations for Film and Video Projects* / Morrie Warshawski / $26.95

Sound Design: *The Expressive Power of Music, Voice, and Sound Effects in Cinema* / David Sonnenschein / $19.95

Stealing Fire From the Gods, 2nd Edition: *The Complete Guide to Story for Writers & Filmmakers* / James Bonnet / $26.95

Storyboarding 101: *A Crash Course in Professional Storyboarding* James Fraioli / $19.95

Ultimate Filmmaker's Guide to Short Films, The: *Making It Big in Shorts* Kim Adelman / $16.95

Working Director, The: *How to Arrive, Thrive & Survive in the Director's Chair* Charles Wilkinson / $22.95

Writer's Journey, – 2nd Edition, The: *Mythic Structure for Writers* Christopher Vogler / $24.95

Writer's Partner, The: *1001 Breakthrough Ideas to Stimulate Your Imagination* Martin Roth / $24.95

Writing the Action Adventure: *The Moment of Truth* Neill D. Hicks / $14.95

Writing the Comedy Film: *Make 'Em Laugh* Stuart Voytilla and Scott Petri / $14.95

Writing the Killer Treatment: *Selling Your Story Without a Script* Michael Halperin / $14.95

Writing the Second Act: *Building Conflict and Tension in Your Film Script* Michael Halperin / $19.95

Writing the Thriller Film: *The Terror Within* Neill D. Hicks / $14.95

Writing the TV Drama Series: *How to Succeed as a Professional Writer in TV* Pamela Douglas / $24.95

DVD & VIDEOS

Field of Fish: *VHS Video* Directed by Steve Tanner and Michael Wiese, Written by Annamaria Murphy / $9.95

Hardware Wars: *DVD* / Written and Directed by Ernie Fosselius / $14.95

Sacred Sites of the Dalai Lamas – DVD, The: *A Pilgrimage to Oracle Lake* A Documentary by Michael Wiese / $22.95